# WICCA AWAKENS

GW00691658

A Beginners Guide
to the Practical Aspects
of The Old Religion.

Re-formatted & Extended Edition.

# KEITH MORGAN

ISBN 1-872189-20-2

Mandrake Press Ltd © 2000

No part or parts may be reproduced by any means whatsoever without prior permission being sought and obtained in writing from the publishers.

## Mandrake Press Ltd.
Essex House, Thame
Oxon. OX9 3LS
ENGLAND

# CONTENTS

# ABOUT THE AUTHOR

*Keith Morgan was born in Cheshire in 1961. He studied various Occult teachings from the age of 11 & was initiated into the craft of the wise in 1977.*

*He continues to work as a practising High priest of Wicca, & as a publisher & author in many esoteric fields. He writes in a simple & concise style which is easily understood by both the initiate & the student of the occult arts.*

*Keith is proud & outspoken about his beliefs, he has given interviews on local & national TV & radio & continues to be in the forefront of developing new ideas about all Occult teachings & paths.*

*Keith is also the editor of The Deosil Dance, the most radical of all Pagan & occult magazines around today*

*Anna Greenwood*

# INTRODUCTION

This book has been specifically written for newcomers to the concept of Paganism, Wicca and the various "Occult" fraternities and societies that exist today. This does not exclude folk who are already well established upon their chosen paths, who may find this book of use as a reference point. It has been written in a concise manner, with the sole intention being not to over glamorise, nor dramatise the practices of Wicca (Witchcraft, as it is known more generally), as they are no more out of the ordinary than the various folklore groups, such as Morris Men, Mummers etc. who still practise their ancient crafts.

This book is not meant to be the last word on Wicca, nor is it the only way of doing things correctly, as so many other authors claim much to their detriment, but is a way of working with the natural magickal energies, with the forces of nature and not along side of them. It is not a book of spells, or rituals that have to be followed to the letter, it needs something else adding to make it a personal reflection for you, they are your time, commitment, faith and understanding, if you have all of these commodities to give to the Old Religion, you will benefit from this book. In a way, this could be looked upon as a first book on the Old Religion, but must never be looked upon as all you will need to know, this is but the first step back to the Ancient Earth Religion of Albion.

Read, Learn, Enjoy, CONTRIBUTE!

## *INTRODUCTION TO THE 1992 EDITION.*

Well it has come a long way since it's initial conception has Wicca Awakens. This book & the response that it has received from people wishing to learn about the craft has been most inspiring, in that the good wishes of so many thousands of readers spurred me onto writing more & more about the Craft & related Occult matters. Once again, as I was re-setting the book via a Desk Top Publishing package I took the opportunity to add more information that I thought would be useful to the beginner.

I would like to take this opportunity to thank you for buying this book & I hope that it inspires you to study more about the Old ways, & to perhaps read more of my works, which are all available from either the shop where you bought this book, or from the address at the front of this book, where a catalogue is available.

# Chapter 1

# THE CIRCLE AROUND THE FIRE

Around the blazing fire, the wise ones sat, their faces warmed by the flames, from the biting cold of the Autumn evening. Cloaks wrapped tightly kept the evening chill from their bones, and flapped silently in the breeze around their backs. High above them, an owl hovered silently, and wolves howled in the dark forests on the slopes of the hills. For one short moment, which seemed to last an eternity , no-one spoke, as the inbred fear of this creature crawled across their minds.

The Wise woman who was the leader of those gathered spoke to the Chieftain of the tribe:-
"The Old Winter's sun will soon be creeping over the hill that is our land, and his death will slowly be upon us, there will be great hardship and much death amongst our tribe, this is our fate that we will follow his death, even the Goddess sleeps beneath her hard white mantle, resting until Spring, and so we must be like Her, conserving our strength until our march across the Great Plains".

The Chieftain listened intently and immediately gave the order for plans to be put into motion to prepare for the hardship, the families must be protected by the warmth of the fire, which must be kept burning continually in the huts, the young warriors were sent into the forest to gather suitable timber, they were also told to keep the skins of any animals killed on their quest, to keep people warm during the winter. Only by their unity and forward planning would they have the resources to be able to survive the harsh winter, as forecast by the Wise One.

An imaginary fantasy concerning an Ancient tribe of people, the imagery may be a dream but the people and their situation did exist once, not as a tribe of people from another land of say 400 years ago, but as a Celtic tribe living in these lands 1,800 years ago. This is where the Modern roots of the Old Religion have some earth upon them, in the wisdom accrued by the Wise Ones around that fire. Not so much the fire that lay in the hearth, but the fire that still burns within the Heart of many men and women today.

They are the descendants of the Wise Ones of the Celts, and it matters not that the above pathworking was set in these lands. All peoples of all races who have and share affinities in the Old Beliefs have within their own ancestry a history of Wisdom, they are followers of THE OLD RELIGION, and have been called by men, most wrongly in many circumstances, WITCHES.

It is these people today who are quickly creating the tribal systems of the New Age, be they classifying themselves Witches, Shamans, Wiccans or Pagans. The names may be different but the path is the same, and that path is nothing more than being a link with the energies of the Old Ones, the Lord and Lady.

The story above was a Celtic pathworking, but the same spirit lives through all tribal systems. Saxon, Nordic, Germanic, even Afro-Carribean culture has a Pagan ancestry, the only thing that changes is the names of the God and the Goddess of each culture. It is the same spirit that is being invoked, only now in a different way, but the same spirit.

The tribal systems are now lost due to the destruction of the tribal identity of the old Traditions, they are now being reclaimed by New Age philosophers, who reject many of the concepts of today's society, and their modern religions of restriction, and go towards the light at the heart of the fire, the pure white light of truth. There have been many lies and falsehoods and many accusations made against the followers of the Old Religion, but their beliefs will always shine through. Many people are now answering their call, rejecting totally the ways of the new gods for a more natural and holistic way of being and belief, that belief being in the Gods and Goddesses of ancient times, the deities of the Woods Lakes, Rivers, Trees and Stones, but never "Devils" as many persecutors have stated. For the persecutors followed the way of the new "Sun god Jesus", working in his name to rid the lands of all Paganism, and establish his church and ministry. They used the image of the perfect man to commit great evils and tell many lies to the world about Pagan beliefs. Pagans never worshipped devils, but in the warped politics of the persecutors, the Pagans had to go. They represented the essence of freedom and the truth, they did not fit into the web of lies spun by the spiders of death.

Witches, or WICCA, as is their correct name, were never totally eradicated, they were just quiet for 300 years or so, until the shouting ceased. They then emerged once more to continue as they always have done, in a way of harmony and wisdom with Nature, since the time when Man lived in caves and looked up in wonder at the Great Moon and the millions of stars within the night sky. It is in this simple spirit that people are once again returning to, and putting faith in, the Old Ones.

It is in this spirit also that this book is written, as a guide through the many and confusing paths of the Dark forest to guide the seeker, not to a ready made religion, but to help him or herself discover for themselves the wonder and beauty of the Lord and Lady of the Old Religion, in fact, to guide them back to the spirit of their ancestors. The only danger that lies upon that path of the seeker is the fact that if they truly find what the seek, they will be more holistic within themselves and be far more able to judge the man made world with its lies and deceit, with the understanding of a Wise One, and they may not like that which they see........
be prepared within yourself and if ever uncertain do not journey back to the Wildwood, for there the Laws of Nature are infinitely stronger that the Laws of Man.

# Chapter 2

# WICCA AND THE RIGHT TO IT

Alone in her small cottage, the Witch sat, fear racked and tormented her frail body, she did not think that one day "they" would come for her! She had always tried to help her neighbours, for she knew that power lay within the herbs that she used, in ways taught to her by her own Mother, and her Mother's Mother before her. She knew that there was no harm within them, how could there be? She grew them herself around her cottage, and she understood the Powers of Nature. But, more than anything, she understood the true nature of the God and Goddess ; she did not like being called a Witch, and had laughed it off many times, but not now......

For seventy summers, since the day she was helped from her Mother's womb, by her own Grandmother, something she could still remember, she had lived in the same village, never going more than ten miles in any direction out of the village. She had trust in her neighbours as she once knew that the trusted her, until the strangers in black came.....

"She gets her power from the devil", one said, (a concept no one knew until the strangers brought it, for in this village there was no church nor minister, it was far too small for that).

"She dries your cows of milk, and feeds that milk to her imps" said another.

"She is a Witch and she must die", said their leader, a hard vicious man, whose sole pleasure was money, especially the 10 sovereigns he would get for this pitiful woman.

Was it any wonder that, being told such tales, the villagers were afraid of the old lady? They strangers were better educated than themselves, they were men of the world, they knew better about these kind of things, it is better to leave this in their hands.....

Now they came, like the wolves of old, feared and hungry for blood, ready to take the children into the night... These wolves were out hunting a special child, the Child of the Goddess.

Tthey crept around her cottage like vermin, trying to see where she was. The door was well locked and barred, they would have to smash it down to get to their prey, they would have to go and get tools from the Inn, they would have to earn their blood money tonight!

The Witch knew that her time had come, and she knew that her allotted time was drawing to a close. She was pleased that this night was the time of the Full Moon, and that it was momentous that it would be on a night such as this that she would be returning to the Great Earth Mother, the Goddess, to be with those old ones who had gone before, resting in peace until it was their time once more to walk this earth as she had done so many times before.

She knew of the Magick of her herbs and after burning her special book, and other items of great importance to her, so they would not be defiled in the hands of her hunters, she took her concoction that she had prepared earlier, and then she unlocked the door, and lay on her bed waiting for the wolves to return.

By the brave and selfless death that she had chosen for herself, they would be cheated of their prey, she would never betray the Goddess and Her Children by consorting with the wolves, and giving the old secrets away... She had known that her time was near, and she had chosen her own exit, far better to keep pure your highest ideals, and strive ever towards them. She had returned home to the Womb of the Great Mother and was happy and at peace..... and what happened to the wolves, I hear you ask? *Who cares!*

When accused of "Witchcraft" in times past, the accused person had two options, either take their own life and keep safe any secrets that they had, or secondly, submit to the torture of their oppressors, thus maybe extending their life slightly. The second option was a vain hope, as capture and accusation resulted in a certain death, as their was a great deal of money involved in payment for the finding of a witch, all funded by the Christian church. The true wise ones realised that it was better to take their own lives and to return to the Goddess, in a painless manner, rather than be tortured to death, or humiliated in a public hanging. It was for these reasons that many of the leading Witches of the time took their own lives, the "Witches" that we read of in the witch trials of 350 years ago were not all Witches, some were just eccentrics who lived in a twilight world of their own fantasy all their lives, and now all of a sudden they were the centre of attention, probably for the first time in their lives, and people were actually listening to their rambling. Is it any wonder that they confessed to the lies and allegations put upon them?

They were celebrities, and for the first time in their lives they were being noticed. This is why the actual reports of the time are not to be taken as fact as to what exactly happened, they were all written from an oppressors' point of view, and not that of the followers of the Old Religion.

Despite all of this, the Old Religion survived, as it is seen by many as the folk heritage of the ancestry of a person possibly carried forward to future generations in the genetic make-up. This may be conjecture, but one thing is evident, more people are returning to the beliefs, values, and ideals of the Old Religion.

This is the way it should be, as with anything that is worth knowing, people have a right to it, to once more get to know and understand the Goddess and the Horned fertility God, as their ancestors once knew them.

Witchcraft, or, as I have already stated, Wicca is the correct name, is a religion based upon the worship of the natural forces around us, the name Wicca comes from the Saxon root word "Wicce" meaning either a wise one, indicating the wisdom that the Priests and Priestesses possess, or in its other form, "Wicasa", it means to bend or manipulate, pertaining to their manipulation or swaying of the natural forces around them, in their Magick, casting of spells, divination of the future etc. Before the Saxon invasion of England, the Wise Ones were just acknowledged as such, natural healers, prophets and soothsayers, of the localised and isolated communities. When asked of their faith, they only claimed to be followers of the "Old Religion" to distinguish it from the "New Religion" of christianity, being brought here by christian missionaries.

The Wicca, unlike the christians, believe in not one almighty god, but two deities, a God and a Goddess. They represent the male and female life force and energies found in nature that are essential for survival. The God and the Goddess were accepted in all Pagan lands, all over the world, from Scandinavia to Egypt and all in between.

In these lands, the God and Goddess were known by many names, and all connected with the Great Folk legends of these lands. It does not matter that the names of the God and the Goddess changed from one land to another, this was the indigenous peoples' way of individualising and personalising the God and Goddess force so they could understand it more readily. The Wise Ones in all lands were the teachers of the wisdom to the Pagan congregation, so the images had to be put over to them in a way which was easy to understand and accept. Therefore, different attributions were given to deities for themselves. This gave the appearances that in Paganism, there was a pantheistic approach to their deities, and that there were many Gods and Goddesses. This is not strictly the case, they were merely aspects of the same male and female forces put forwards in a personalised way that was acceptable to the people.

It was always assumed by outsiders to the Old Religion, since the 15th century, that Witches worshipped the devil. This is not the truth, but in the politics of the Papal hierarchy of the time, this was used to exterminate the rebellious nature of the continuing Old Religion, and to enable them to bring more money into the churches.
 In fact, when the first missionaries came to preach their religion in these lands, it was taken by the Pagans of the time that the " Jesus and Mary" images were compatible with their own beliefs, with the concept of the "Son of God" being the new "Sun God" and with more than a little adaption being given to the virginal status of his mother.

Both the Old Religion and the New Religion existed in relative harmony with each other until the political stance of the establishment changed, and they saw Wicca as a threat to their own status.
 The persecution times were a terrible time and much suffering was taken by the Wise Ones at the instigation of the christians, with between 9 and 14 million people accused of Witchcraft and murdered accordingly in Britain and Europe. This has always been unacceptable and unforgivable and thanks to the changing of ecumenical law to civil law, it will never happen again, as the church has lost its power of life and death decisions.
 Everyone in the world has a right to believe in whatever religion they choose, free from persecution from any quarter, and since the repeal of the Witchcraft Act in 1951, it is perfectly legal to believe and follow the practise of the Old Religion

No one has the right to prevent you from following whatever faith you wish, and this was reinforced by the United Nations in their Bill of Human Rights, which states in Article 18:-

*"Everyone has the right to freedom of thought, conscience and religion: this right includes the freedom to change his religion or belief, and freedom either alone or in community with others, in public and in private, to manifest his religion or belief in teaching, practice, worship and observance."*

As you can see, it would be against both civil law and moral conscience for anyone to deprive you of your right to follow the ways of the Old Ones, the persecution times have ended and you are free to follow your beliefs.

# Chapter 3

# THE GODDESS & THE GOD

The main aim of the practice of the Old Religion, is the worship of the Lord & Lady, who are the God & Goddess. This is through giving praise & thanks to them for helping you through the struggle of life, unlike other deities of other religions, who see the existence upon the earth as a suffering process, the God & Goddess regards all Pagans, be they Wiccan, Shamans etc as their children & let no harm come upon them.

To the Wicca, the Goddess is the Great earth mother, that is planet earth, & the God is the force that moves upon it, powering the Earth , as the Earth powers the force, both giving & taking from each other, in fact, a creative sexual union. As the Moon was once part of the Earth, the Moon is looked upon as being a Goddess image,this is the daughter of the Earth Mother, protectress of the Night, & the people of the Earth who are in attunement, with the Earth , she looks over the Earth whilst the Earth sleeps. She is a force that is Young matronly or old, as her differing phases dictate. When the Moon is waxing she is the young Maiden the seductress, with her awakening sexual charms, the creative spirit that is awakening. At the full of the moon she is the full fertile Mother, the same as her own Mother, from whose body she came from, as do we all. When the Moon is on the wane, she is the Old crone full of the wisdom of her ancient path, that which is to be learned & offered to all that can take it.

The Goddess has a great affinity to all Ladies, as her Luna cycles correspond with that of Women, on a 28 day cycle, she reaches her peak at the full of the Moon, as the woman reaches her peak at ovulation. The full of the Moon is regarded in Wicca as a meeting time, a time for the Coven or group to gather in praise of the Great Earth Spirit, reflecting in her daughter, & ask her aid in any problem. This is summed up perfectly in Charles Leland's book Aradia ; Gospel of the Witches, Aradia being the name of the Daughter of the Goddess sent to Earth to teach mankind the art of Witchcraft, in the legends of Tuscany.

*"When I have departed from this World, & whenever ye have need of anything, once in the month & when the moon is full, ye shall assemble in some desert place, or in a forest all together join to adore the potent spirit of your Queen , My Mother Great Diana, she who fain would learn all sorcery, yet has not won its deepest secrets, them my Mother will teach in truth all things as yet unknown & ye shall all be free from slavery, & so ye shall be free in everything, & as a sign ye are truly free, ye shall be naked in your rites, both Men & Women also.*

The nakedness or as it is called in Wiccan circles, being 'Skyclad' was a symbol of the followers of the Old Religion showing their freedom, it was also a way of removing the stigma of poverty, all being equal & all being seen to be equal within a coven meeting, both rich & poor alike. The other reasons for being skyclad were of a sexual nature, namely, one of the main ways of raising power, was by consenting couples privately performing sexual intercourse known as the Great rite, & by being skyclad, it was an indication that they were free & what better way to express , & indicate the pleasure that it gives, as well as being able to make love to your chosen partner within their presence. I must stress that it was usual for this to be at outdoor meetings where those gathered would take their respective partners into the privacy of bushes etc, nowadays, this ritual sex, known as the 'Great rite',is only performed by established sexual couples,within the confines of their own privacy,it is not license for an orgy!.

Wiccans realise that being Skyclad is a way of cutting yourself off away from the constrictions of society, & that as such & when practised in a ritual setting dedicated to the fertility of Beast, Field, Nature & Man, & when your life depended upon that fertility, then it was perfectly natural act. The words of Aradia were an oral tradition handed down from one generation to another, they were seen as the asking of the Goddess for the state of nakedness, as in a recognition of the natural state that mankind should be in.

The image of the God is seen as the image of the Maleness of nature, the reproducing entity needed for the fruitful union with the Great Earth Mother. He is pure Male sexuality, horned & hoofed, to represent his lustfulness, (not with any Demonic connotations, that concept belongs to a newer religion). He is the beast of the field, the Goat, the Ram, The Stag whose only function it is for the procreation of the species, so it is with the Horned God.

He is Pan to the Greeks, the Goat-foot God of the Paradise Arcadia, & Cernunnos to his early Celtic counterparts, & like the Goddess has many names & symbols, Herne the Stag Lord of the forest, Osiris the Horned eternal Father of the Egyptians, Apollo, the God of the Sun etc, but with one consistent thread running throughout, he was always the image of Light, the compliment to the Earth & the Moon, THE SUN, Totally necessary for the existence of life.

In the Summer months, he is the Lord of the Land, the Fertility God of the Fields, John Barleycorn & his fertility is within all aspects of nature. In the dark Winter months he does not physically die, his spirit lives on in the Darker aspect of Herne, the Stag Lord, the God of the Hunt, who appears as the Sun wanes at the Winter Solstice, he is still vital to the well being of the tribe, as the provider of food.

The only food available in the winter, being other animals, mainly to eke out the Summers harvest, thus as the hunter, in the Dark Months, the Stag Lord, becomes the hunted.

Both God & Goddess are equal within Wicca, it is a dualistic faith, with one complementing the other & as we their children upon the Earth must recognise ourselves as the representation of the respective deities upon the Earth, according to our own sexuality, we carry that spark of divinity within us from the deities. As ancient man had to unify himself with his God & Goddess, he communed with them under names of power so he could call upon them in whatever land he resided in, & on the particular occasion that he needed the aspect of a particular deity. The concept of many names is still common within the Old Religion, with different people using different names, this has given way to the concept that there are many deities within the Old Religion, there aren't, there are many traditions of the Old Religion, & they use different names for the Lord & Lady; Following on, there is a small list of some of the names most commonly used in Modern Wiccan circles, for the different aspects, of the God & Goddess always remembering There is only One Goddess & one God, but many aspects in many traditions of many lands.

The union of the Horned God & the Goddess is utmost in the concept of the union of positive & negative, Male & female, Yin/Yang, in a gesture of magickal expression, this is Wicca!

# GODDESS NAMES.

ANDRED; The name of the Goddess in the South east of England

ASTARTE ; Babylonian goddess of Love & Lust

ARIANRHOD; Welsh Mother Goddess, Mother of Llew

ARADIA ; Italian name of the strege (Witches) goddess, a female Version of Hesu, born of a union between her mother & her brother, far more ancient is the concept of the Divine trio being Father, Mother, Daughter. Aradia assumed human incarnation to teach the craft on the Earth.

APHRODITE ; The Greek Goddess Of love

BRIDE / BRIGID / BRID; The Goddess of Spring Christianised into St. Brigid

BENZOSIA; French Goddess name, meaning unknown.

CEREDWENN; Celtic Goddess of Inspiration & keeper of the Cauldron.

DIANA / DANA; Mediterranean name for the Luna Goddess, & leader of the wild hunt also known in Eire as Dana, meaning,' of the De-Danaan'

EPONA;Celtic Goddess whose symbol was a white Horse

GAIA; Early Greek name for the Great Earth Mother

HABONDIA; The Lady of love.

HOLDA; Nordic name for the Goddess.

HERTHA; Goddess of the Home.

HERODIAS; Possible derivation of Aradia, as It is a name for the Daughter of the Goddess

ISHTAR; Mesopotamian Goddess akin to Astarte

ISIS; Great Mother Goddess of the Egyptians

IAMBE; Daughter of Pan

LILLITH; The archetype of Women's Sexuality

MA'AT; Egyptian Goddess of Justice.

NICNEVAN; The Pictish Witch Goddess.

MORRIGAN; The Welsh Goddess of the Sea & Death

OLWYN; Celtic Fertility Goddess.

PERSEPHONE; Greek Earth/Underworld Goddess

VENUS Roman Goddess of Springs & Vegetation

VESTA Roman Virgin Goddess of Fire.

# GOD NAMES.

ANDRAS; The compliment to the Goddess Andred
CERNUNNOS; Gallic & Celtic Horned God.
DUMMUS; Mesopotamian consort of Ishtar.
DIANUS; Romani British twin headed God, with 2 faces, one looking to the past & one looking to the future.
DAGDA; Celtic God, Literally, 'the Good God'
GWYDION ; Welsh bardic God of wisdom.
HERNE ; Saxon name for the Horned one, a God of wisdom & woodlands. A Guide to the underworld, leader of the wild hunt in Britain
LUCIFER ; Not a demon but a light-bringer. Also means morning star which could be a reference to the planet Venus, which can also equate with the Goddess Lucifarnus.
LUGH/LLEW Name used all over the British Isles & Eire for the Sun God.
JANUS ; As Dianus.
PAN ; Greek fertility God.
JOHN BARLEYCORN ; 'Light of the Fields' British fertility God.
JACK I'TH GREEN ; Folkloric Fertility God.
OSIRIS; The Father image of the Egyptians.
ODIN; The God of the Norse, who symbolised great wisdom after hanging upon a tree to obtain the wisdom of the Runes.

NOTE: Once again I really must stress that the outlook on the Old Pagan deities is neither Pantheonistic or Monotheistic but should always be considered as a duality.

The names that I have ascribed to the above dual deities or deities within a cycle are not the complete list, there are any many more from many different traditions.

# Chapter 4

# WITCHCRAFT TODAY
# WHAT IS HAPPENING.

## IDENTIFYING PATHS

The various groups that exist within the Occult world today reflect the entire spectrum of belief within one or two particular systems, be it cabbala, Mysticism, Egyptian religion, Nordic religion or Wicca. As well as many other groups that combine some or all of the above to formulate their credo. As well as that which is structured their also exists people whose do not rely upon other systems of magick or beliefs as an aid to packing out their own thinking with second hand philosophies & instead turn to the voice of the wind or feelings from the heart, as they are the real instructors on natural magick, not some Guru on high in their ivory tower. It is within this spirit that I originally formulated this book not to recapitulate what has already been said, so many times by so many authors, nor to erect a sacred pedestal for myself, as so many others have attempted to do.

This book was established to give the seeker, new on the path, the truth & that is, the best teachers of an ancient spiritual heritage are the spirits of the woodland & heath who are but images & manifestations of the different aspects of the Lord & Lady.

The next best guide is your own intuition which is the only one which can tell you whether something is right or wrong for you personally, if it feels right, it invariably is!

Wicca & other Occult paths are today in a state of fragmentation, with splinter groups emerging from more mainstream groups to fulfil peoples needs on a far greater level than the established groups may be doing. All religions & religious groups, serve the same means, the worship of the deity in a personal way, & the feeling of unity with the individual members of that group on the same common grounds. One of the first confusions that you may come across when you start your search for your ancestral roots will of course be the way in which you will in future, relate your philosophies to your life, or the way of working your magick that you will be most at home with.

In Occult terminology this is classified as your particular path, or the way that you follow, & believe me there are a myriad of ways & as much diversification of thought as there are Pagans, Witches & Occultists

Once you have decided upon which role it is that you can relate to then it will be shown to you which will be your particular path it is that you will follow.

Using the following guide, as an indication as to the mainstream traditions that are around today & you will obtain an indication as to the tradition that you will be most comfortable with. As the main tenet of this book is to show you how to get started within Wicca, it is obvious that a greater concentration will be given to Wiccan groups.

TRADITIONAL WICCA - View Traditional Wicca as a source, rather than a tradition. It is a source of many other later traditions root material, in that it has been borrowed heavily from & as such has taken on the shape of many of the later traditions which has been instrumental in borrowing from the source.

The main aspect of inspiration of Traditional Wicca comes from the pre Christian cultures of the world & as such a lot of the symbology & deity base stems from these earlier pre Christian religious beliefs.

Traditional Wicca is claimed to be the Most Oldest branch of the Craft as it takes its inspiration from the many Folklore customs of our ancient ancestors.

GARDNERIAN WICCA - The tradition that is claimed to have been founded by Gerald B Gardner, described by many as being the father of modern Wicca, however their is much evidence to prove beyond a doubt that Dr. Gardner was indeed an initiate of a traditional Coven, & piecing the fragments together formulated a complete system that exists today. This traditions the one that many of the tabloid press picked up on in the 60's for its naked rites, & orgies! True Gardnerian rites are often Skyclad, but like so many groups there are bone fide reasons for this, as for the orgies, well no one I know have ever attended such!

The use of the title Gardnerian Witchcraft is something of a misnomer, as Initiates of this system (of which I am), simply prefer to call themselves, Wiccans, Witches or members of the Craft! the term Gardnerian is used by outsiders to describe these practises.

HEREDITARY WICCA - a branch of Wicca originally orientating towards traditional branches of Wicca, however with later traditions developing all the time, it is now taken as being a tradition passed down within a family system.

It is not so much of a group but more of an extended family. If someone claims to be a hereditary Wiccan this means that it has been passed on from parents or Grandparents. As time progresses & with interest being shown in the old Religion today, descendants of todays Witches, if following their parents path will be able to claim hereditary lineage, then perhaps it will not be the big thing & sadly a term of one-up-manship that it is seen as being used as today!

ALEXANDRIAN WICCA - The system of Wicca based upon the creation of the late Alex Sanders, self proclaimed King of the Witches! Alex, gelled together a combination of Cabbala & Gardnerian Wicca & formed his own system, despite unsubstantiated claims of initiation by his grandmother! He had what seemed to be a certain charisma of his own & through sensationalist media hypes in the mid 60's, following upon the persecution of Gardnerian groups of the time, he introduced a lot of people to his own brand of Wicca & by doing so, opened the concept of Pagan worship out to a lot of people who would not have normally come into contact with it. It was by far the most easiest group to become a member of, as people were initiated not on merit, but rather by volume to increase the membership at a stroke - not a good ideas really!

DIANIC WICCA - A women only group focusing totally entirely upon the Goddess aspect of Wicca with the total rejection of both the Horned God & the male aspect of divinity. A true & total tradition of Matriarchy, established in direct opposition to the patriarchal dogma of Christianity, but as it has established a dogma of its own, it goes to show that two wrongs do not make a right!

ARCADIAN WICCA - Arcadian Wicca like Dianic Wicca is a relatively new tradition, in that many gay men are being attracted by the strength of the Horned One, & as such are gathering to worship him. This is far more of an attunement for gay men to concentrate upon the strength & power of the phallus of the Horned one, rather than the dualistic belief in the fertility cult that is mainstream Wicca which is based upon the sexual union of God & Goddess, it is particularly harmonious when seen to be balancing out with Dianic Wicca (see above).

SEAX WICCA - Very modern invention of Saxon Wicca, circa 1974. Invented by Raymond Buckland in his book 'The Tree', a very bad mish-mash of ideas previously held & adapted from traditional & Gardnerian sources.

MODERN WICCAN MOVEMENTS - Wicca is developing constantly & this is a good thing, when something remains static, it stagnates. Wicca is so flexible it can be easily wrapped around todays life & is able to relate to the relevant points that living in the 20th century throws at us. Certain newer movements are emerging on what seems to be a weekly basis, some will stay the course of time, some will fall by the way, one cannot give a full listing of these newer 'traditions' as it is an ever changing scene,
    With the mainstream Wiccan paths, we have the addition or assimilation of other Occult paths, a lot of which tend to be assimilated with Wiccan paths, much of which is not really compatible, including the Judaic, Christian & satanic paths, these outside influences to Wicca include;

PRIMITIVE BELIEFS / NATIVE BELIEFS / SHAMANISM. BABYLONIAN / SUMERIAN / EGYPTIAN CLASSICAL TANTRIC CELTIC / NORDIC - All of the above are just a few examples of pre-christian traditions which were based upon a synthesis of belief established around a duality of male & female divinity. Starting with the earliest forms of worship of the old pagan deities, the Sun & the Earth & the Moon & the Stars, which developed as per differing cultures into the respective deities that we now associate with those particular cultures. This is the melting pot of modern aspects & theologies of Wicca as we now know it, & as Wicca is developing, we are once again returning to these earlier traditions after a half century of contamination by cabbalistic interruption.

GNOSIS - Gnosis can only be described as being the Occult or hidden face of the heretical Christian church, which viewed mans role as part of the great universe in a completely different way to mainstream Christianity

JUDAIC / CABBALA - Cabbala, is the Gnosis of the Judaic faith, in that it is a spiritual path aligned with the Judaic belief system. It is the occult tradition of the Rabbi's, who were entrusted with the names of power of God. Cabbala is often associated with traditions of Wicca such as Gardnerian & Alexandrian systems, however more opinion is giving credence to the rejection of Wiccan association with the Judeo Christian cultures of Cabbala & Gnosis, & returning once again to the pagan deities of our ancestries such as Celtic, Saxon & Nordic, in the British isles, & native American shamanism, which is a worldwide culture.

**ALCHEMY** - the medieval search for the unknown, & a quest for knowledge & spiritual enlightenment, with the theory of bringing the Gold of Knowledge out of the base elements of the world. Immediately totally misunderstood as being alchemists having devilish pacts etc but was without doubt the fore runner of todays science of Chemistry.

**GOLDEN DAWN** - A system of magick & magickal tradition based upon Cabbalistic, Classical & Egyptian orientated occult traditions

**O.T.O / A. A./ THELEMA** - an offshoot of the Golden Dawn, formed at the beginning of the century & starting with the O.T.O.. The A.A or Astrum Argentium was started by the Magickan Aleister Crowley, who devised his own system of Magick based upon earlier pagan traditions of all types, with a smattering of Cabbala. Crowley has often been associated by his critics as being a 'Satanist' or a 'black Magickan', but there again so have I & we all know you shouldn't listen to rumour don't we?!!!!

**CHAOS** - Chaos magick is the invention or realisation of a small group of people, in Britain in the early 80's who assimilated a belief system based upon the surreal mythos of the dark aspect of literature & the void of creation, along with the 'pseudo sci fi legendary' of writers like H P Lovecraft etc, whose imagination certainly fired off a spark of creation, that gave way to inspiration.

**SATANISM** - Nothing to do with Wicca or any other Pagan culture, as Satan is the opposition to the good of their saviour Jesus. As Christianity has nothing to do with Pagan pre Christian beliefs then it stands to reason that neither has Satanism.

**CHRISTIANITY**- Not valid at all to be combined with any Pagan beliefs; even early Christian Missionaries used some kind of raw associaed symbology toinstigate a cover up & eventually a total suppression of Pagan beliefs. Anyone who says that there canbe such a thing as a Christian Witch is a fool in that they do not understand their own Pagan heritage, & by trying to fuse two incompatible system s together, they are relying upon a crutch of an earlier belief. TO BE A WITCH, YOU HAVE TO HOLD PAGAN, PRE - CHRISTIAN BELIEFS

As you can see, choosing your path is one of the most important decisions that you can decide which is for you. It is not so much the factual evidence of antiquity that matters, but the spirit & affection behind the revival of the worship of the Old Gods & Goddesses. It takes a great deal of thought & meditation as to which path or tradition òf an occult vein is for yourself. Of course you may decide to embark upon what may well turn out to be the wrong path, we all do it.

I once studied the Cabbala for 5 years until I realised that Gods Phone number (which is how I viewed cabbala as a series of magickal numerological correspondence), was not available. At this point I decide that I was certain that it was the equality of Wicca was the path for me, & I proved myself right.

However, I do not think it could be said that I wasted 5 years studying cabbala, how could I have wasted It, I still have the knowledge of such & whilst it has nothing to do with the traditional branch of Wicca that I later studied, & which I now follow, it gave me an excellent grounding in establishing a psychic map of the universe through the cabbalistic tree of life & gave me an indication, as to the workings of the Cabbalistic system of magick.

You cannot claim to be a Witch or even a Pagan if you cut yourself off from the nature of your surroundings be they a woodland, a heath or a beach, as long as the surroundings are natural, then there is a place to commune with the God & Goddess, not some obscure ritual enacted out of an equally obscure book in a bedsit in the centre of a city. This is because the structured rituals that appear in books are only someone else's way of communication with the forces of Nature, what you need is your own rituals, devised & created by you, from your knowledge that you have amassed in your studies & what is more, rituals that actually mean something to you!

To do this, what I propose to do, is in the rest of this book, lay bare the essential facts & give the information necessary to you to construct your own first simple rituals using symbolism that has always been sacred to the Goddess & the God.

Rituals are mankinds way of marking important events in life whether it be an initiation, a funeral rite or simply the marking of the Sabbats to show the turning of the Year (in an ideal world this should be a matter of intuition & knowledge of the natural energies around you & not be in need of rituals that tell you what is happening in the natural world that moves round us!), in short rituals are needed by us to indicate the passage of life & show the attainment of wisdom

If you choose to create elaborate rituals taking hours in some secret temple, fine. If you equally decide to create much simpler rituals to be worked in some wood, such is equally valid, even if you decide to work all your rites through imaginary thought processes (pathworkings). It is all up to you & as such is your responsibility, as long as you get close to the spirit of your belief,as long as your ideals are pure in thought & as long as you aspire to be back with the Old ones, then you cannot fail in your quest!

The following symbolism will be of great use to you in creating & devising your own personal system of working & philosophy of getting back to the Old ways of worship. keep notes on your learnings & assess everything for yourself, calling upon the Goddess of the Wise crone for any assistance required.

# Chapter 5

# THE WITCHES YEAR

The Sabbats of the Old religion are the marking times of the turning of the year, they mark the passage of the year & the changing of the seasons, they are times of sadness & joy depending upon the season, but always times of reflection on that which has gone & for that which will be. There are eight Sabbats in a year & their dates are;-

| | | |
|---|---|---|
| Samhain | ; | October 31 |
| Yule   ( Winter Solstice ) | : | On or around December 21 |
| Imbolc | ; | February 2 |
| Eostra ( Spring Equinox) | : | On or around March 21 |
| Beltane | ; | April 30 |
| Litha  (Summer Solstice) | ; | On or around June 21 |
| Lughnasadh | ; | August 1 |
| Modron (Autumn Equinox) | ; | On or around September 21 |

For the correct dates of Solstices & Equinoxes, please consult a reliable Almanack or Magickal diary, such as the Deosil Dance Magickal Diary available from where you bought this book, or direct from the publishers at the front of this book.

I will lay out very briefly what each Sabbat means for the majority of todays Wicca, though many groups have their own interpretations of the symbology of each season, depending on how they can relate to it themselves.

SAMHAIN: The Celtic New Year. Samhain is the feast of remembrance for all those who have gone before to the Summerlands (the resting place on the astral Planes for all Wicca).

YULE:  The mid Winter celebration of the reign of the White Goddess  &  the Stag Lord,  God of Hunting (Both seasonal representations of the God & Goddess).  Yule or Iul is Nordic for Wheel & is symbolic of the turning of the year with the weak Sun gaining in strength after the Long Darkest night, to combat the oncoming coldness of Mid Winter.

IMBOLC: The daughter of spring is born of the White Goddess after her sexual union with the Horned God last Beltane. Although not out of the reign of the White Goddess yet, it is a hope of the spring that is near.

EOSTRA: The beginning of the reign of the Green Spring Goddess, the fertile energies being concentrated into the earth, bringing the Green mantle once more to the forest tree's & the fields.

BELTANE: This is the era of the sexual union of the Stag Lord & the young Green Earth Goddess bringing forth their fertile intentions upon the Earth, a time of sexual awakening of the Magickal energies within.

LITHA: This is the height of the reign of the Green Goddess bringing her aspects to bear on the fields & the harvest. The Lord of the Wildwood, the Foliate Man, is into his reign, powered by the energies of the strong Sun.

LUGHNASADH: The feast of Lugh (Or Llew), the Fertile God, the year is now on its wane, dark aspects now creep into the Magickal processes of the Earth. Doubts as to the abundance of the harvest. Deep doubt & serious prayer to the Goddess for aid, as she transcends from her transition from Green Goddess, into a mature, fertile Mother Goddess image,(portrayed as a Golden Harvest Goddess).

MODRON: The Gold of the Harvest colours appear in the woodlands, & the Golden Goddess is well into her reign, In the fields, the Harvest is now gathered in, much to the praise of the Goddess, Corn Dollies are made in her honour, & sacrificed under the plough, as it prepares the ground for another year. She has taken part in the Magick of the season & prepares to take on her new role at Samhain, that of the White Goddess. The Lord of the Wildwood is also prepared for his transition into the Stag lord at Samhain, ready for a seasons hunting.


As well as the Sabbats, there are the Esbats in the year, they are the nights of the Full Moon, & there are 13 in one year.

These are working times, as Sabbats are celebratory times, using the Magick of the occasion to help people with spells or to initiate new members into a group. If you practice the Old Religion alone, rituals on a full Moon can aid your personal development, as you will be working with the natural & full energies.

The Luna Calendar of 13 cycles is also very important to Pagan cultures, the Moon is the Guardian of the night, the Goddess (or Daughter of the Goddess), is seen to be protecting her people, in the dark hours.

The full moon was always chosen as a time for folk to gather in the outlying areas of habitation, for two reasons, one spiritual and one practical. Firstly practical, in the days before decent roads, with a certain amount of lighting, it was far easier for folk to walk to their Esbats, over large distances, across fields & rough land, with the light of the full moon to guide them, even today in parts of the countryside, the full moon is known as the Ladies Lamp.

The spiritual reason was that folk understood the ebb and flow of the Luna cycle and if Magick was to be successful, it was far better to work with the creative tides, particularly when the cycle was in a static state, this gave the dark of the moon for acts of banishment and the full of the moon for acts of Good Fortune.

# Chapter 6

# THE SYMBOLS OF THE CRAFT.

As with all other Magickal systems, there are Hidden wisdom contained within the symbols used in rituals & for adorning the equipment used, in the creation of Magickal talismans, spells etc. Given below is a comprehensive collection of the most widely used symbols.

THE PENTAGRAM: The five pointed star of protection, symbolising the universe & its components, the 5 elements of life. Fire, Earth, Water, Air & Spirit. The pentagram is used to invoke at the start of a ritual & for banishing at the end. Each element has ascribed to it an invoking & banishing Pentagram, so they can be used in elemental rituals. An inverted pentagram is the symbol of 2 initiation.

THE HEPTOGRAM: A symbol used to illustrate the universe as viewed from earth, namely the 7 planets. Not as widely used as the Pentagram & does not contain the same protective powers, which are ascribed to the number 5 not 7. It cannot be used as an invoking or Banishing aid for protection in any circumstances.

THE HEXAGRAM: Cabbalists use a system of Hexagram rituals as invoking & banishing aid, for planetary rites, but again due to the absence of 5, the protection given by the pentagram is not there. Far better usage is made in Celtic cultures, as a solar symbol. In one particular Solar ritual, Morris men, lock 6 swords together in a clear symbol of the Sun.

WICCAN WHEEL: The 8 Sabbats of the year also the so called eight paths to wisdom.

THE TRIANGLE: Symbol of the trinity of Mother Father & Daughter. Also used inverted as a 1 initiation symbol. Two triangles, one correct & one inverted also symbolise Male & Female energies & the adage 'As Above; So below' A triangle & a pentagram is the symbol of 3 initiation.

THE CIRCLE: Again a universal symbol of the infinite, but also a symbol of life, never ending, & without beginning & without end. When drawn with a strike through it, this is the symbol of the Magickal circle, & can be written as such.

SYMBOL OF THE GODDESS: It can also be used as a Horned God symbol in Traditional circles, but generally indicated the Goddess.

THE ARROW OF POWER: The symbol of the Horned God moving forth upon the Earth Plane; it indicates that the power never stays still & is in continual use.

THE SYMBOL OF THE GODDESS: Often confused with a Hebrew Aleph letter, it is a symbol of the Crescent Moon rising over the Earth.

WAXING & WANING MOON: Used to invoke the powers of the Moon Goddess in these phases.

THE 'SALUTE & SCOURGE': Often described as such in Gardnerian & Alexandrian systems, they are in fact symbols of both Male & Female, the perfect couple.

As well as the symbolism above, it must be remembered that Natural symbolism such as Tree's, Crystals, Plants, animals also have potent uses within Magick. Ancient megaliths etc are also to be regarded as symbols of male & female deities. Phallic symbols such as Menhirs (standing stones) are dedicated to the God, whilst Gateways such as Dolmens & Henges, are the symbols of the Goddess, as are sacred wells & hills often with Cairns upon them, which indicates that the hill is a place of ancient worship.

Returning once more to the Pentagram, below are the banishing & invoking Pentagrams for all the elements, always draw them in the direction of the arrow, visualising burning Gold light as you draw them.

INVOKING             ELEMENT             BANISHING

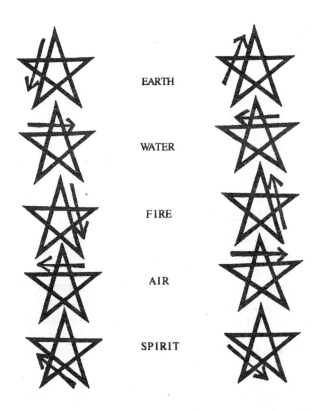

EARTH

WATER

FIRE

AIR

SPIRIT

# Chapter 7

# A WITCHES TOOL CHEST

Whilst no Paraphernalia is needed to hold a belief in the God & The Goddess when practising rituals in their praise, you may find need for items of equipment to represent the elements either symbolically or in essence. You can make most of the equipment mentioned in this chapter, using my book MAKING MAGICKAL TOOLS & RITUAL EQUIPMENT, or you can purchase it from the many suppliers that are now in existence supplying tools especially designed for the pagan & occult communities.

Do not buy tools that have been designed for other specific occult paths, such as Pentacles that have symbols from the Cabbala etched upon them, as you will be distracting your energies from that of your intended worship, the pagan deities, not Jewish ones!

There are many craftsmen around today who will make your equipment for you, provided that you give them full details of what you require. Of course it is far better to make all your own equipment, thus forging a personal link with your tools but to some people it just is not viable.

ATHAME;   As well as being the personal tool of the witch, the Athame equates with the element of Spirit & is the first tool the newly initiated Wiccan is presented with at their initiation. It is pronounced ATH-AY-MEE  & is used within the circle for the casting & invoking & banishing rituals, for Charging spells, talismans etc. It is never used for cutting outside of a magickal situation. The Curfane is a white handled knife that is sometimes used for cutting or carving as in candle Magick, but some consider this to be a Cabbalistic interference & not intrinsically Wiccan. The Blade of the Athame is of steel (though some belonging to Priests & Priestesses have been known to be of silver), & the handle black (or have black upon it), made out of Bone or wood, Horn or bound leather, in fact anything that is natural that you feel happy with.

PENTACLE: The Pentacle is the next tool the novice is introduced ·to, it is the symbol of second degree initiation & links in with the element of earth, as it is a Female tool.

It is also a protector, due to the inscribed Pentagram upon its face. It is used in Craft circles as a diffusing element when something is being charged, i.e.; other tools, spells, Talismans etc. It is placed upon the Pentacle so as to safely diffuse any excess power. It is also used as a banishing agent to remove other peoples influenced from any Magickal object. It does not matter what the Pentacle is made of, as long as it is of natural origin, such as Wood, Slate, Copper, Brass etc. Silver is a good metal to use as you would be invoking the aid of the Luna Goddess into your pentacle which would fit very with with the symbolic nature of the Moon within the Craft. The inscription upon the Pentacle must be pictorial & not contain any words, whether in magickal alphabet or not. It must be a pictorial symbol of your understanding as to the Nature of the Goddess; God & your expectations & beliefs within the craft. Use any of the symbols in the previous section, but arrange them in a way that means something to you, combining them with any symbols of your own division, or aspects of nature that are significant to you.

WAND: Wands are not intrinsically Male or female, but can be designed to take on the appearance of either feminine or male symbology, with Phallic or Vulvic attributions. The correct length for a Wand, is from the Crook of your elbow up to the tip of your middle finger. Wands must be made of wood, & can be decorated to suit the person who owns it. The wand corresponds with the element of Air.

CHALICE: Definitely the Most feminine of all the tools, equating with the element of water. It is the grail of the arthurian legends, the cup of inspiration, a smaller version of the Cauldron of Cerridwen. It is shared with all participants in the ritual, within the one circle, no matter of rank or position within the group. At the ceremony of the Cakes & Ale, held at all Coven meetings, the Cup is passed among all celebrants, each taking of the Wine, Mead, Cider or Beer it contains. This is a sharing of all the gathered, all being equal. The cup is passed from male' unto Female & vice versa, & always with a Kiss, to express the Love each Witch has for each other.

SWORD: This is a symbol of rank within a Coven, used in the same was as the Athame, to cast & banish circles but also as a tool to direct the energies raised towards any particular purpose. The sword equates to the element of fire & not as in cabbala, with AIR.

It is created under the influences of Mars, forged in steel, the metal of Mars. As it is a tool of rank, only the leader of a coven must use the sword within a ritual.

All magickal tools must be consecrated to their particular owner, & kept away from more mundane objects. It must only be used by the person to whom it was consecrated , & handled by a third party only with the consent of its owner, & definitely by no one to whom you do not have respect for.

As well as the elemental tools, there are other tools that is used within Wiccan circles.

THE CAULDRON: Now quite a rare item as they are very collectable by Wiccan & non Wiccan alike. The traditional cauldron was a large 3 legged pot ( 3 being the number of the Moon Goddess), made of iron with a bale handle. It is a symbol of feminine wisdom & the giver of knowledge. In Welsh Folklore was kept by Cerridwen. This notion of inspiring knowledge is something that is kept alive today & cauldrons are still used for meditational purposes, scrying, as with a crystal. To obtain a reflective surface to scry in, fill the cauldron two thirds full with water, consecrate with salt & use in the same way as a crystal or dark mirror.

THE BESOM: Along with the cauldron probably the most widely recognised symbol of the Old Religion that the majority of the general public relate to. In actuality, the Besom is a Phallic staff (a large version of a wand) that had the phallic end disguised in times of persecution, with broom or heather, thus making it into a Besom. It was probably never used for mundane cleaning but was kept separate for magickal uses. One of the ways that a Besom was used, & one that is documented, was by a Female Witch, who would smear the shaft of the Besom with hallucinogenic Flying ointment, she would then straddle the shaft rubbing it along her vagina that way allowing the hallucinogenic properties of the ointment to enter her. So strong is this ointment containing many poisonous plants, that it would have proved fatal if ingested & the way of the witch of medieval times was a far safer way of allowing it in to their bloodstreams. The ointment is so potent it induces a coma state for 8-12 hours in which the person using it has fantastic hallucinations of attending various rituals.....this was the basis of the belief that the Witch flew to the Sabbat upon her broom, when in reality she never left her cottage.

ROBES: Robes may be worn in ritual, but are not essential, only if modesty forbids the 'Skyclad' state. If robes are chosen to be worn,it is better they are loose & free flowing so as to not inhibit movement. The material used should be a natural material such as Cotton, Wool or if possible, Silk. The Colours of your Robe should correspond with your own personal equating with that colour.

THE BOOK OF SHADOWS: This is a holy book to the Craft, containing instructions, spells, information etc. It is not holy in the sense of taking every word contained within as Gospel, but more of respect for the wisdom of the ancients which it contains. It should be looked upon as not being complete, & can be added to & personalised by the Wiccan whose book it is. The book is traditionally kept in the personal handwriting of the owner. The reason for this, is that it bonds a personal link with the owner to the book, as well as, if one has to laboriously write something out, they stand a better chance of remembering it, than if they were to simply read it.

JEWELLERY: The use of Jewellery within ritual is ancient indeed, it stems from a belief that the wearing of precious metal & stones invokes a power over the wearer. When this is coupled with the said metals & gemstones being inscribed with magickal symbols, this latent power is greatly intensified, & can be used in a Magickal direction by the wearer. All Lady Witches wear Necklaces that is kept only for ritual use, as images of the Goddess were portrayed wearing necklaces, as a feminine symbol of the Craft. Though its the rule that Ladies wear Necklaces,many Men also wear ritual lamens/Necklaces for the beneficial & magickal effects described above. Along with Necklaces, Bracelets & Rings are favoured among pagans & Witches of all Traditions. The wearing of a Magickal symbol in every day life is not only a public affirmation of your beliefs, but a protector (Using pentagram symbology), & a beacon showing to those who can interpret the symbol that you are what you are, thus keeping you in contact with other Pagans.

All Magickal items, or items used for Ritual, or are special to you, should be kept apart from any generalised objects that you have around your home. If it is possible to keep your magickal tools in a chest,or box, away from prying eyes or unwelcome touching, this way you keep your energies imposed upon your tools, & keep them Psychically clean, & personal to you.

# Chapter 8

## RUNES GLYPHS & SIGILS

When compounding talismans or spells etc or for writing down records of rituals & magickal workings in your book of shadows, you may find it advantageous to use a magickal alphabet. By doing so, your concentration upon an unfamiliar system of communication is intensified, & as such your concentration upon the end result is also heightened.

Runes are one of the most common magickal alphabets used. Some are Nordic in orientation, some, like Coelbran y Beirdd are Celtic, & other Runic systems such as the Runes of Andred, are a modern interpretation, but equally as valid, as being one Wiccans interpretation of a Magickal alphabet. It is possible to assemble your own Magickal alphabet. This is not as difficult as it may seem, after all what is an alphabet, but a collection of symbols that relate to a characteristic of a sound used in language. For example, the letter o could be used as $\mathcal{O}$ ; by following a pen along a paper whilst vibrating the guttural sound of the letter through your body. The whole alphabet using this system, is laid out below in the Lunic alphabet. By producing magickal alphabets in this manner, you are creating personal magickal bonds with the alphabets of your own creation, & it will be easier to relate to them in a magickal sense.

LUNIC

A   B   C   D   E   F   G

H   I   J   K L   L   M   N

O   P   Q   R   S   T   U

V.   W   X   Y   Z

*Please*

# THEBAN SCRIPT

A  B  C  D  E  F  G

H  I  J –  K  L  M  N

O  P  Q  R  S  T  U –

V  W  X.  Y –  Z

# CELESTIAL SCRIPT

A  B  C  Ch  D  G  H

I  K  L  M  N  O  P

R  S  Sh  T  Th  Tz  V  Z

# COELBRAN Y BEIRDD.

A  B  C  Ch  D  DD  E  F

FF  G  Ng  H  I  L  LL  M

N  NH  O  P  PH  R  Rh  S

T  Th  U  W  Wh  Y

# OGHAM.

Ogham is a sacred Druidic alphabet that was used for putting inscriptions upon the top & side of stones, staves etc & was read by running the first & second fingers along the top & edge of the stone through a 90 angle

The centre line is the edge of the stone, one part of the glyph was written upon the top & the other down the side.

A-+ ·· B -ᚱᚾᚷ C-ᛁᛁᛁᛁ- D-ᛁᛁ-- E -ᚻᚻᚻ F-⫻-G-⫽--·H--ᛁ·---

I--ᚻᚻ- J-ᛁᚱᚾᚾᚾ-M--/-- N-ᛁᚷ-Ng-⫻·-O--ᚻᚻ--·P--X··Q-ᛁᛚᛁ--

R-⫻⫻- S-ᚦᛏᛁ-·T--ᛁᛁᛁ--- U--ᚻᚻ·-- V-ᚾᛏᛏ··

## ANGLO SAXON RUNES.

F ᚠ   U ᚢ   Th ᚦ   O ᚩ   R ᚱ   Ch ᚻ   G ᚷ   W ᚹ

H ᚻ   N ᚾ   I |   J ᛄ   E ᛁ   P ᛈ   Z ᛦ   S ᛋ

T ↑   Be ᛒ   M ᛗ   L ᚻ   Ng ᛝ   Ö ᛗ   D ᛞ   a ᚪ

ae ᚫ   Y ᛡ   ea ᛠ

Small letters are soft.

## MAGICKAL SIGILS.

   A magickal Sigil is a way of condensing & encapsulating a short piece of information, corresponding to a particular deity or symbolic entity, either a God form or Planetary energy. The most widely known series of planetary sigils are cabbalistic in origin & are not really compatible for use within Pagan traditions of Magick. A far better system is achieved by using any alphabet including the standard ABC the Sigil is devised by writing down all the letters of the Deities name or names, or magickal intention for a spell. Remove all the duplicated letters so only one of each is left, then combine the letters in an artistic manner to form the Sigil. To hide the meaning further if this is desired, or if the meaning is apparent, it can be embellished with extra symbolism pertaining to its meaning.
Example;- ARADIA:
Remove 2 A's so all is left is A R D I.
Combine all the letters to create a Sigil thus
Add extra non letter symbols to achieve the finished Sigil.

34

# Chapter 9

# BASIC WICCAN /PAGAN RITUALS.

Many Witches & Magickans (correct spelling) use many magickal tools in their craft, have special rooms or temples put aside for the use of magick only, as a simple practitioner you do not need these elaborate items (unless of course you wish to)

There will be some ritual items that you will need, such as candle holders, candles, bowls, Incense, plus your Magickal tools all of these can be obtained from reputable Occult suppliers or you may wish to make your own equipment (see my book MAKING MAGICKAL TOOLS & RITUAL EQUIPMENT for information on this), or you may have these items already in your home. Before the ritual assess what you will need & gather them together, your magickal tools, the correct colour of candles, Incenses & Oils, Charcoal, Incense burners etc

If you are going to be using items that you already have at home, it is always wise to Magickally cleanse these items, using Magickal cleansing Solution. This is a collection of herbs that are renowned for their Psychic cleansing properties, it is a simple case of rubbing this solution over an object to remove any traces of past influences (see chapter on Incense in this book for details of how to make this Cleansing Solution).

Each of the Magickal exercises in this book tell you precisely what you require for each one, along with this, you will also need access to;
A small table with white cloth which you can use as an altar.
Two white candles with Holders to be used as Altar lights to give you some illumination.
A simple white robe, which you can work your magick in (Like many Witches you may prefer to work naked in your magick, or as we call it skyclad!)
& the most important requirement, Absolute Privacy! - Privacy is needed so your train of concentration will not be disturbed in your magick. THIS IS IMPORTANT! Witches cast circles to keep energy in, Magickans cast circles to keep spirits out, as you will not be invoking Spirits, a circle of this nature is not needed,

though you will need to keep your energy in & directed to the purpose of your ritual.

## USING EQUIPMENT FOR MAGICK
The candles, Incense, Charcoal etc that you use, like everything else should have been obtained for the purpose & not been used for anything else (all magickal items are available from where you purchased this book or you can make your own)

CAUTION: CANDLES, INCENSE & CHARCOALS ARE A FIRE HAZARD, PLEASE ENSURE THAT INCENSE BURNERS HAVE A LINING OF SAND BEFORE PLACING THE CHARCOAL IN, & THAT ALL CANDLE HOLDERS ARE STURDY.

Candles used for Candlemagick should be left to burn out to activate the spell, & it should be one spell per candle, no candle should be snuffed & used again. The most ideal situation is one where you can leave the Altar set up with the Candles & incense burning, & be left to go out on their own. REMEMBER THEY ARE A FIRE RISK, & ENSURE THAT NOTHING FLAMMABLE IS NEAR EITHER CANDLES OR INCENSE BURNER.

If your incense Burner has a lid, use it. If you have got a small clay tile to place your incense on, even better, because it will insulate it against you Altar.

REMEMBER, EVEN AFTER 4 HOURS, THE CHARCOAL CAN STILL BE VERY HOT, DISPOSE OF DOWN THE LOO, OR IN THE GARDEN, WHERE THEY WILL NOT COMBUST WITH ANYTHING ELSE.

As I mentioned earlier, the best rituals are the ones that you formulate for yourself. This task of writing your own rituals can appear daunting to the beginner, so to give you some idea's as to format, I have included in this chapter some very basic rituals that you can use & expand upon. All these rituals can be performed indoors or out in a secluded spot.

All rituals of all traditions usually have the same basic format that follows as such;
1; The opening Ceremony
2; The content, Intent or purpose of the ritual
3; The closing Ceremony

The opening & closing ceremonies are usually the casting & closing of the Magickal circle.

The Magickal circle is a barrier & a boundary upon the Astral Planes that exist upon an equal parallel to the Earth Plane that we exist upon. The circle is a combining link of the worlds of Man & Spirit, a narrowing of the veil that separates the worlds so mankind may attune to the spirit worlds & vice versa, so the Spirit world may be attuned to this our world. Within Wicca the circle is a barrier to keep power raised in the ritual in close confines with the magickal act being performed. It is not the same as a Cabbalistic circle which is composed as a fence to keep out any demonic entities

The ritual of casting a Magickal circle is done to create a magickal working environment for the practitioner. This environment can be used for consecrating Talismans, spells, pouches etc, or the ritual itself can be designed around a ritual to invoke the energy of a particular deity or influences of a particular Planet (see my book PLANET MAGICK for details of this).
The Magickal circle can be used to work Magick in, cast spells, consecrate equipment etc. The correct format of a ritual for performing a consecration or spell etc should be performed as following.
CONSECRATION OF WATER & SALT
OPEN THE CIRCLE.
INVOCATION OF THE DEITIES
CONSECRATION OF THE ITEM
CLOSE THE CIRCLE.

PREPARING TO CAST YOUR CIRCLE
Directions for casting a circle, are as follows. To create your sacred space, for casting your circle, make sure that the room you are working in is not dirty, or cluttered, or contain anything that may distract you, close curtains, even in daytime to avoid outside distractions, remove phone from hook, make sure you will not be disturbed.
Have your purification bath, wash your hair (use bath purifier & Ritual shampoo rather than soap, they contain herbs & oils that have magickal properties that will cleanse the spirit) dress in your robe, or towel dry if working skyclad.
Clear yourself some space to move in, about 8 square feet, place your altar in the centre of the space, with everything that you

need upon that Altar. This will include Water & Salt in suitable containers; Athame; pentacle,; Wand; Incense Burner; Chalice; Charcoal & Incense (choose an Incense to correspond with the work in Hand) You can now light your candles & incense & prepare to cast your circle

## DRAWING THE CIRCLE
Take the Athame & Draw the circle staring in the east, visualising a flaming circle surrounding you.

## CONSECRATION OF WATER & SALT
Place the Water vessel upon the pentacle on the Altar, & pour the salt into it. Place the Athame into the water & say ;-
*"Blessings be upon thee O creatures of Water & Salt, protect all that you touch, Guard & protect against all Evil & pour forth good Intent. This I ask in the names of The Old Ones......& ..... (Inserting the particular God & Goddess names you use).So mote it be!"*

Take the vessel of Salted water around the circle starting from the East saying;
*" I consecrate this boundary between the worlds of Mankind & Spirit, with this essence of the land & the Sea, let it bless, purify & protect. So mote it be!"*

Take the Incense around the circle starting from the East saying;
*" I consecrate this boundary between the worlds of Mankind & Spirit, with this essence of Fire & Air, let it bless, purify & protect. So mote it be!"*

## THE INVOCATION OF THE ELEMENTS
Take the Athame to the East & draw a pentagram of Invoking Air, whilst saying ;-
*" Guardian Spirits of the East, Guardian Spirits of Air, Protect your domain within this realm of this circle; be it a good barrier remove harm & concentrate good In the name of the Lord & the lady................................; So mote it be!"*

Take the Athame to the South & draw a pentagram of Invoking Fire, whilst saying ;-
*" Guardian Spirits of the South, Guardian Spirits of Fire, Protect your domain within this realm of this circle; be it a good barrier remove harm & concentrate good In the name of the Lord & the lady................................; So mote it be!"*

Take the Athame to the West & draw a pentagram of Invoking Water, whilst saying ;-
" *Guardian Spirits of the West, Guardian Spirits of Water, Protect your domain within this realm of this circle; be it a good barrier remove harm & concentrate good In the name of the Lord & the lady..............................; So mote it be!*"

Take the Athame to the North & draw a pentagram of Invoking Earth, whilst saying ;-
" *Guardian Spirits of the North, Guardian Spirits of Earth, Protect your domain within this realm of this circle; be it a good barrier remove harm & concentrate good In the name of the Lord & the lady..............................; So mote it be!*"

The circle is now cast & is ready to be used within the greater part of the ritual. To cast a circle is something that you must absolutely know off by heart, so practise this exercise so you will become word perfect & totally efficient at casting a circle.

THE CLOSING RITUAL
After any Magickal working has been performed the circle will need banishing or closing down so as to not litter up the Astral Planes with unwanted Psychic energy, as uncast circles act like a beacon at attracting all manner of elemental entities.

To close down a circle again, start at the East & proceed around the circle, this time in a Widdershins (anti-clockwise) direction, drawing the respective elemental BANISHING pentagram for each quarter saying;
*"Guardians of the East (or North, or West, or South), I thank you for your aid in this Ritual, Depart to your elemental realm of Air (Or Earth, or Water, or Fire) & rest again until you are summoned once more. In the name of the Lord & Lady.............& ............. Hail & farewell!"*

When this has been done, go to the Altar & draw a banishing Pentagram of Spirit over it & say
*"This rite is over, let all who came as friends in peace, depart as friends in peace. So Mote it be!"*

Extinguish the Candles & Dispose of the Water & Incense

## CONSECRATION RITUAL.

When you are consecrating any piece of Magickal equipment , as you must, before use, to build a personal bond with that tool up), you are both charging that magickal talisman etc or piece of equipment with your own energy & placing your personality upon it, thus making it unique. below is a short ritual that is to be used within a circle to enable you to make personal to you all your equipment which you must consecrate before using in a circle. The following consecration ritual is to be performed within a circle.

## CAST THE CIRCLE

Place the Magickal item to be consecrated upon the Pentacle & say;-
" I CHARGE THIS MAGICKAL TOOL, WITHIN THE ELEMENT OF EARTH TO ASSIST ME IN MY MAGICK TO THE GREATER PRAISE OF THE LORD & THE LADY
SO MOTE IT BE.

Sprinkle with consecrated Water & salt & say;-
" I CHARGE THIS MAGICKAL TOOL, WITHIN THE ELEMENT OF WATER TO ASSIST ME IN MY MAGICK TO THE GREATER PRAISE OF THE LORD & THE LADY
SO MOTE IT BE.

Hold the tool in a candle flame (Not too near if combustible) & say,;-
" I CHARGE THIS MAGICKAL TOOL, WITHIN THE ELEMENT OF FIRE TO ASSIST ME IN MY MAGICK TO THE GREATER PRAISE OF THE LORD & THE LADY
SO MOTE IT BE.

Hold the tool in the Incense smoke & say;-
" I CHARGE THIS MAGICKAL TOOL, WITHIN THE ELEMENT OF AIR TO ASSIST ME IN MY MAGICK TO THE GREATER PRAISE OF THE LORD & THE LADY
SO MOTE IT BE.

Hold the Tool aloft & say;-
" (GODDESS)........, & (GOD) CHARGE THIS TOOL WITH YOUR POWERS FOR ME TO USE WITHIN THE ARTS OF MAGICK. IF I MISUSE THE POWER FREELY GIVEN TO ME WITHIN THIS TOOL MAY IT TURN AGAINST ME TO MY END. SO MOTE IT BE!"

Present the Talisman etc or tool to each of the quarters starting with
the East, in a Deosil direction, saying;-
" Spirits of Air, Recognise this tool of power & give my Magick
your aid."

Go to the south, & say ;-
" Spirits of Fire, Recognise this tool of power & give my magick
your aid."

Go to the West, & say ;-
" Spirits of Water, Recognise this tool of power & give my Magick
your aid."

Go to the North, & say ;-
" Spirits of Earth, Recognise this tool of power & give my magick
your aid."

Wrap the newly consecrated tool in silk or cotton, & keep with the
rest of your magickal tools.

CLOSE THE CIRCLE

# Chapter 10

## WORKING TOGETHER FOR THE GOOD OF THE CRAFT

The best way to practise the Old Religion is with a group of like minded people within a group situation. This need not be a structured coven working the ways of one of the traditions described earlier (though this is obviously the best way forward, as you will be learning the Craft as it has been taught within that group). You could get together with a few like minded & dedicated friends all thinking in the same direction as yourself & wishing to worship & give praise to the Goddess & the Horned God in the unity of a group. By careful discussion among yourselves you will be able to work out what appeals to you, equally so, you will be able to discuss what does not appeal & what you may object too within a group situation.

On the other hand, you may wish to shun the idea of working within a group situation & prefer to work out your own ways of working as a solitary Wiccan. This is equally as valid as a group situation with like minded friends, & the idea of self dedication may suit you rather than a formal initiation into an established Coven, we will discuss this later on in this chapter, but first I wish to point out the benefit & downfalls of joining an established group & then leave it up to you to decide which is YOUR path!

The benefits of joining an established group or Coven are as many as the disadvantages but to elaborate they are, & by no means are these lists complete;

1; The feeling of unity to a like minded group of people, you will become one of an extended family of people, all meeting together in Perfect Love & Trust.

2; You will get first hand experience of group workings

3; You will amass the group knowledge, making the job of sorting out conflicting ideas easier for yourself. As the group will already have an established set of ideas or tenets laid down, the groundwork of research will have already been done for you.

4;You will get immediate help from the elders of the group as well as practical help in your studies & magickal workings & practises.

5; You will become part of a group identity & fit into the circle of people that are gathered in a way that links your magick with theirs, & be able to identify your magick with theirs.

6; You will not have to purchase outright all the books & equipment you many need to start with, though you will be expected to contribute to Coven funds.

7; As you have been taught, so will you be able to teach & you will, in time, be able to lead your own group, & initiate as you have been initiated.

The disadvantages of joining groups could be;

1; Finding the wrong group of people who do not hold the same ideals as yourself.

2; Being a newcomer in a group situation is difficult & rising up the ladder to leadership is hard.....but extremely rewarding & worthwhile. Sadly however, some people with inflated Ego's cannot take to it, preferring to have the Craft served up to them on a plate.

3; You cannot locate a group in your locality that you can find that takes in newcomers for instruction

Upon reflection, the benefits outweigh the objections but it is entirely up to you, the individual & if you feel that it would be better not to join then so be it! that is your decision & you need not be excluded from the worship of the Goddess & Horned God, a self dedication ritual is equally as valid for the person working alone as an initiation would be for a working group.
    THOUGH IT IS IMPORTANT TO REMEMBER; That within a group situation, the person performing the initiation is an initiate themselves & are passing on their gift of initiation. It is not possible for a person who has undergone a self dedication, or self initiation to then initiate people at will & 'Initiation' of this manner seldom work leaving the would be initiate out on a limb.

VALID INITIATION, LEADING TO GROUP LEADERSHIP & THE RIGHT TO INITIATE OTHERS EXISTS ONLY FOR PEOPLE WHO HAVE BEEN INITIATED THEMSELVES BY ANOTHER PERSON!

However there is no need for the would be seeker to feel excluded & alienated, Wicca is at long last coming out into the open & being recognised as a valid religion, therefore it is possible to show your allegiance to the Lord & Lady by your self dedication to them. This is not a cop-out to initiation & should never be used as one, but a showing of allegiance to the Old ones. You are placing your affirmation upon the Astral planes for all of the Spirit world to see. This is your commitment, your inclusion into the outer circle of the Craft of the Wise.

If in future you are given the opportunity to be initiated THEN DO IT! Your commitment of earlier will be taken as a token of your level of devotion. The ritual that follows however is not one of initiation, but dedication & even though it is not an initiation it is still a powerful & solemn rite & undertaking to uphold the good name of the Craft & to promote it always. Remember ONCE A WITCH, ALWAYS A WITCH!

The equipment that you will need for the following ritual include. White candles Charcoal & Incense burner Banishing Incense & Initiation Incense & Oil Wand; Pentacle & Athame Chalice & wine, beer or cider Robe & white cord (optional) Bracelet Ring or Necklace Salt & Water (In Bowls) Purification bath Statues or pictorial representations of the Goddess & the God.

## A SELF DEDICATION RITUAL

This ritual is to be performed on the Night of the Full Moon. When you have prepared your work-site, temple etc & have erected your Altar with all the necessary equipment to the North of your working Circle, prepare a bath using the purification mixture (see Chapter 12) & whilst taking the bath reflect upon the ritual ahead & its intentions. Are you sure that the commitment ahead (for it is a commitment) that you are undertaking, is a solemn undertaking for life? have you any worries or misapprehensions?

If so then go no further, for you will not be sure within yourself & that could be disconcerting within a ritual situation.

If you are sure that you have understood your commitment then enter the work area skyclad, for this is to be your re-birth into the Craft of the Wise (if the ritual is to be held outside, situate the site near a water source for the bathing, you may also dispense with the purification bath is bathing is done with running water such as a river or stream, to take the negativity away from the body).

Burn Banishing Incense to clear the working area if needed.

CAST THE CIRCLE

Place initiation Incense upon the charcoals, place your left hand upon the Pentacle & say the following declaration.

I..... (your chosen Magickal name) Wish to petition my Lord & lady of Light upon this hours to witness my intention to follow in the ways of all the Old Ones who have come before me over the Astrals, to worship your existence within the Universe.

I totally understand that I make this request entirely of my own choosing & free will & that after this sacred night, I will be known to all as a follower of the old Religion, A Pagan & A Wiccan.

I will defend the name of the craft & the Might of your power with my life, If ever I stray from this oath then I will forfeit this power. I swear that i will let no Man or Woman speak ill of the Old Ways.

I am a standing stone within a universal circle A protector & defender of the divine faith, not following the words of a man but that of a Goddess & a Horned God.

I am a free man/Woman, I have shed the burden of the world with my cloak, I am naked before your sight & I am not ashamed.

This is the first day of my Life & I am re-born!

Take the initiation Oil & anoint the body in the following places; In between the eyes. Each Nipple The Bottom of the Spine The Genitals

Take the chalice of Wine, beer or cider & consecrate it, by placing it upon the pentacle, placing the Athame into the liquid & saying;

A toast to the old ones I am with you As you were with me in the beginning So mote it be for all times.

Consecrate your Ring, necklace or bracelet as your symbol of the acceptance of the Old ways, & wear it as your symbol of membership to the outer circle of the Craft.

Hold the wand above the altar & say;

With this stave do I protect the craft So by this stave will the Craft protect me!

BANISH THE CIRCLE.

The rite is over & you are now a dedicated Wiccan & member of the Outer circle.......BLESSED BE!

Of course there is far more to being a Pagan, a wise one, a Witch, whatever you choose to call yourself than performing one ritual on the Night of a fall Moon. This is the beginning of a way of life that will take you into many strange area's. Working with a group makes for easier study & being part of a group you will be told what is expected of you to learn & to study. You may be asked to specialise in certain area's or skills, such as making Incenses & oils (as I was asked), or you may be asked to learn he tarot for the rest of the group to consult, or you may be asked to become the scribe for the group & write up all the group records.

To give you some idea, what is below is what is expected for you to study from the point of a Traditional or Gardnerian point of view, each Coven will be different & ask you to study different things, for example, an Alexandrian Coven may well ask that you study Cabbala, that is up to you, but from a strictly Craft orientated point of view this is what you should learn & should know at each degree.

FIRST DEGREE.
The Knowledge of the Ritual tools; The Knowledge of the Sabbats & Esbats ; Witch law or ethics.; Pagan deities ; Craft History ; Craft Symbolism ; General tarot symbolism ; Opening & closing circles with help ; Creative visualisation. ; The study of a clairvoyance technique.

## SECOND DEGREE.

Increasing tarot Knowledge ; The use of Crystals for scrying ; Use & preparation of simples ( Herbal remedies) ; Use of the Ritual tools Use of Magick ; Use of simple spells ; Opening & closing of circles unaided

## THIRD DEGREE.

Conducting Rituals ; Initiating rituals ; Esoteric Tarot ; Use of magick mirrors ; Astral projection ; Herbal aphrodisiacs Compilation of Incense & perfumes ; Introduction of Tantra (Sex magick.)

Within Alexandrian circles an Initiate is claimed to be a priest or Priestess from the Initial Initiation. Within Traditional/Gardnerian Covens, a priest or Priestess is an extra title conferred at a ritual that is extra to the First Degree, it coming in at second, so extra knowledge that a Priest or Priestess should know would contain;-

Officiating at rituals ; Leading the Coven ; Sorting out disputations Initiating New Members ; Creating Unity ;Contacting of Higher beings ; Practice of Tantra ; High plane projection ; Tarot or Clairvoyant adept.

All of this is just within the confine of the Craft, outside of this, you should also be taking an interest in World affairs & their significance on the Craft, such as the protection of Mother Earth & her many children, Ecology & Green issues. Your outlook as a Pagan is now of a holistic nature, viewing the whole world as your concern & not just your own back yard, you have sworn an oath to protect the earth & this is what you must do. In fact ecological pressure groups, Animal rights groups etc now have many Pagan cells or organisations set up within them to cater for Pagans wishing to Join.

Becoming a Pagan, or realising that you are a Pagan means returning to a set of values that mankind used to live by before the advent of structured Chaos. It is a harmonising with the earth & her powers. Try to harness this for yourself, from any angle that you feel is right, try top live by the seasons as the Animals do, resting more in Winter to use the natural energies around you in Summer.

Growing or collecting some of your food & storing it, is another way of living with nature, that way you get the best unadulterated food possible, using the old methods of gardening rather than resorting to the use of harmful chemicals, which are both harmful to you & to Mother Earth.

Supporting Pagan projects no matter in what field, is to the benefit of the Pagan community, if we are seen to be creative & caring, it is one step nearer to achieving a good name for the Craft as a whole & to you in particular, & the respect of outsiders to the craft can only be a good thing. This way, Paganism, the Craft & all the associated imagery is going to be established once more as a legitimate belief system & not something that is outmoded or archaic, Demonic or Evil, but a true system of harmonious belief that is not to be feared, but is something that can be at peace with the rest of mankind, if only they would accept it & tolerate it as our way of living, that we have every right to.

Through working for the good of the Planet & mankind, we gain recognition for our good works & acceptability from those on the outside of our Pagan ways, but looking in, observing & waiting for us to make mistakes, then they will pounce upon us, as they did in times past & accuse us of things for which we are Innocent.....remember the burning times may well be just around the corner, be on your guard & stand steadfast for your Pagan rights.

# Chapter 11

# IMAGINARY IMAGERY

Before one can appreciate the technique of performing Magick as a reality, it is a sensible practitioner who gets themselves familiar with the techniques of projecting ones mental images onto the greater dimension - reality!

The practise of the manifestation of an image is the basis of most occult practise, it is not the "duping" of yourself that most critics of the occult decry it to be, Creative visualisation is one of the most important techniques that one can learn, for with it, the positive aspects of magick are put into force, by seeing something,you believe in it, by believing in it you have faith in it, & once you have faith in a concept you know it will work for you - positive magick, plain & simple!

In a ritual context the projection of an image, whether it be an elemental apparition on the outskirts of a Magickal circle, or the existence of the circle itself depends upon two things:-
1; the mental agility needed to bring it forth.
2; the belief in the existence of the Image.

Therefore if you cast a Magick circle omitting the creative visualisation then all you have done is gone through a physical process that is entirely useless without the mental thinking behind it. What is the point of buying a hang glider if you have convinced yourself you will never have the ability to fly the thing. The same exists with Magick, what is the point of knowing how to perform the Magick needed, if you fail to have the confidence to use it to your own good ?

The visualisation of the barrier of the image is the most important process that you can learn, as all Magick exists upon the astral plane & the unconscious mind attired into consciousness is the key to its power. Visualisation may seem to be unimportant to the beginner, but be assured, they are not, they are the basis of all successful magick, bringing forth onto the outer what is the light within.

Certain occult groups/Covens, etc lay great store in pathworkings, that is the concentration upon a series of images cobbled together to create a scene in time or space.

This is excellent as a method of creating the imaginary capability, but where some groups go wrong with these exercises, is they use the pathworking as a ritual within itself, but it isn't, it is merely the exercise aiming towards the final aim....Ritual usage of creative visualisation !

Creative visualisation are very useful in ritual work & to give an introduction into this, I have created a short series of exercises aimed at awakening the creative potential.

## EXERCISE 1   POSITIVE VISUALISATION

This is an exercise aimed at creating the manifestation of the protective Pentagram image. This exercise will come into its own when practising Magick in that you will be invoking & bringing forth an image that you associate with your energy field from within, your Astral body or if you prefer your 'Body of light'

Familiarise yourself with the instructions before starting on the exercise.

Sit in a comfortable position upon a hard backed chair, close your eyes & place your hands flat upon your lap.

Breathe in a regular pattern of holding your breath for 3 seconds & releasing for 3 seconds, continue this until you establish the breathing pattern unconsciously

Open your eyes once the pattern is established & directly in front of you start to visualise the invoking pentagram of spirit. Starting at one line at a time, as you would draw it, when using in ritual, see the lines as blue lines of pure light, not only are you visualising the Pentagram, you must also bring into the exercise the belief in it.

THIS PENTAGRAM ACTUALLY EXISTS, Not only is it your creation, but an expression of your will power, something you have created actually exists.

Hold this image for as long as you can then slowly break it down line by line in a visualisation of the Banishing pentagram of Spirit, which is drawing it in reverse to invoking.

The result of the exercise must be assessed by the Old adage of ;..."Magick being the ability to cause change through the positive use of willpower...". Seen in this context, what your creative visualisation outcome was, is no great surprise, you have exercised your own store of Power, that of mental ability.

## EXERCISE 2    VISUALISATION OF A DEITY

Carrying the experience of the above exercise a stage further, we now approach a high powered Magickal exercise, that of the visualisation of a deity or energy, practised frequently, good results are achieved. The best kind of energy to start with, is one of a planetary or elemental force, this will give you the experience of coming to terms with forces ·outside the normal sphere of consciousness, & will put you at ease with these forces before trying to invoke any of the archetypical Gods & Goddesses.

The procedure for this visualisation is as follows:-

Cast a circle of protection around your working area.

Sit in a comfortable position facing East.

Perform the breathing exercise as above.

To the east outside the circle, visualise an equilateral triangle in pure gold Light, on an equal parallel to the floor, but approximately 4" above floor level.

Within the centre of this triangle, concentrate upon a visualised point of light. Around this point build up an image of the energy you wish to visualise, using all your knowledge of this force, to build up a correct composite picture. To help with this, it may be of use to burn a corresponding incense, or to wear a corresponding oil.

Concentrate upon the image as a whole being & see it as a manifestation of such & of the Astral planes, but most of all, believe in what you are seeing, as a being of the element which is being invoked & as a being of your own magick.

When you find your concentration waning STOP!

The image should have dispersed, if not banish it with a banishing Pentagram of spirit.

After doing this exercise, relax within the circle & think back to the short ritual that you have just performed. What thoughts or image came into your mind whilst you were doing it ? Write down any results (or non results for that matter), keeping a record of dates, times, places, Phase of moon, state of mind, physical conditions of the body, biorhythm etc, if you are a woman, record what stage of your monthly cycle you are in. All of this is to keep an accurate record of your magickal workings, & before long, a pattern will emerge that you will be able to relate to. You will be also able to build up your own lists of magickal correspondence, with regards to deities, energies etc, that will aid you in your rituals in future. Banish the circle.

The whole exercise should take no longer than 30 minutes.

## EXERCISE 3  DEVELOPMENT OF CLAIRVOYANCY

Clairvoyancy, or clear vision, is a force that exists within all of us,& unlike some 'Experts' on the subject, who believe you have to be born with the potential.  I take the view that the ability to be clairvoyant is one that can be learned as easily as reading and writing is for a small child. The following exercise is one that will introduce you to your own clairvoyant skills (the word power is one that I do not use readily for this or any other Occult skill, like anything else, once learned it is not forgotten & can only improve with use) & for the exercise you will need:-

Scrying incense & Charcoal (with burner or dish) A Chalice & consecrated water OR A Crystal Ball OR A dark Mirror. This method is known as scrying, & is simply, expanding your consciousness through a medium of reflection, thus looking into the deeper you, any reflective surface can give good effect, such as a still pond etc, it is a meditational device and nothing more, through these personal meditations, deeper things can be learned.

Cast a circle around you.

Light some scrying incense

Sit in a relaxed manner upon the floor. In front of you place your tool mentioned above, that you will be using for scrying with.

Look into your tool & visualise an invoking pentagram of fire just underneath the surface. Look into the centre of the Pentagram & take note of any visions or coloured images that you see there, you may see it cloud over or not, it is dependant upon each individual & how the clairvoyancy manifests itself through that person.

When finished, banish the Pentagram & close the circle.

This a very simple exercise, but do not underestimate its potency (or any of these exercises potency), as I explained earlier in this book, constructing or adapting your own rituals are the best that you can perform, & as can be seen by my rituals, they do not have to be over elaborate or drawn out to be highly efficient.

As all of these rituals are designed to make you more aware of your own potential, both within a ritual circumstance, if you choose to consciously perform Magickal exercises such as these,so you will increase  your Magickal potential  & this will become more of a confidence for you when performing more in depth Magickal acts, such as spells etc.

REMEMBER : As no one else will benefit from the results, all that I ask, is that you be honest with yourself & the results that you achieve.

# Chapter 12

# GOOD SENSE & INCENSE

It is absolutely vital that in any Magickal working all the elements & equipment used must be in total harmony with each other, for correct Magickal results to be achieved. This includes people & apparatus & equipment, which should all be harmonious with each other, giving the feeling of correctness, a unity with the knowledge that what you are doing, will succeed & will have the desired intention of the ritual. This is a ruling that applies in all magickal systems including Wicca, Cabbala, etc etc.

One of the most important tools that one can use for successful magick is incense or perfume, within a ritual setting. It is important as it gives the whole proceedings the correct atmosphere or feel, especially when one is working with Deities/Elemental & Planetary correspondence, as the Incense prepares the working areas atmosphere, in a manner that is conducive to the invocation to the invocation of a particular force or deity. It produces an environment where the forces invoked feel at ease & where they are welcome, it is their invitation card to the ritual, & they can relate to its correspondence.

With Incense & perfume, you have created an environment where the force is happy, after all, could you live in an alien environment such as underwater, without an artificial aid ? Of course not, & this is why it is vital to use the correct incense for the correct deity invoked.

When buying Incense & ritual perfumes (as opposed to making them yourself) It is always advisable to deal with a reputable company, one that has a great experience that the work requires. It really is not just a case of slapping anything together that seems to fit & hoping for the best. Incense making is a skilled art & should be seen & acknowledged as such, after all, the results of your ritual may hang upon the potency of the Incense, which is the manifestation of the knowledge of the incense maker. The compilation of Incense is complicated & before deciding upon the type of incense to be made, other considerations have to be taken into account.

Things such as;-
The time of the Day; Month; Year
The position of the Planets
The phase of the Moon.
The harvesting of the herbs at the appropriate time.
Having mixing bowls & utensils of correct planetary correspondence.
Making sure that the receipts used is viable.

Only when all these things are satisfactory can you continue with the compounding of the Incense. It is possible to experiment with incenses & perfumes, but remember it is a specialist procedure, & must be taken steadily with no short cuts. With recipes, it is highly unlikely that you will have access to Coven records on incense, as very few exist, & it is always better to avoid books full of recipes, as they are invariably wrong. It is far better to formulate your own recipes using good guides for planetary & deity correspondence of ingredients such as Culpeppers Herbal; My own book s Planet Magick; & Traditional Wicca & Crowley's '777',the best guide of course is your own common sense.

Common sense is vital for it is wise to remember that even by burning, the active qualities of the Herbs, Barks, Oils & Gums, used in your incenses, as released & ingested by the practitioner giving a stimulating effect to a greater or lesser degree, depending upon the ingredients used. As an example, Deadly Nightshade is Saturnine, & Foxglove comes under the rulership of Venus, No one in their right minds, would consider using any of these & others in an incense or Oil ( Unless a one way trip back to the Goddess is the Magickal intention....in which, I am sure it will be a roaring success!)

It has been suggested in many 'Occult' books by 'Noted celebrity Occultists' that such ingredients as Sweat, Sperm & Menstrual blood be used in incenses & perfumes. Whilst this may be agreeable with the animalistic instincts to find these things & their biological make-up arousing at certain times, it is only when they are fresh & on the body. For this reason, these ingredients are very potent & special, they are personal to you & your magickal/Sexual partner, & should never be used in a group situation, as all you will be doing is passing the sexual messages from one person to another, & when these are applied upon Chakra points ( as Ritual perfumes are), these substances can be very consuming & provoking.

A lot of Grimoires give vast elaborate instructions as to the correct collection of herbs for Magick such as;

*"Collect the Vervain, at the third hour of the Full Moon, when Saturn is in Pisces & only from the Hallowed ground of a churchyard"*

This instruction would not make the Vervain any stronger, but because this long drawn out instruction is given, it sorted the dabbler out from the serious practitioner, who knew that the correct instruction was the first part, & the latter part of the command was a blind to deter the uncommitted.

When collecting plants from the Wild, always only take as much as you will need, with the permission of the plant where you are obtaining your specimen. Never use iron in the Harvesting, always leave a portion of the plant intact to re produce itself within its growth cycle. Leave a small gift such as Bread or wine or beer ( leftovers from a Sabbat or Esbat that have been consecrated are especially favourable) & most importantly, Say thank you to the spirit of the woodland, heath or wherever you obtained your bounty.

When using Herbs that you have collected yourself, make sure that they are totally dry, or else they will rot your finished incense.
When mixing incense, mix all the dry ingredients together then add the essential oils to the desired potency, a little at a time. Make a note of all the ingredients & their amounts for future reference. Store all completed incenses in Sealed glass jars for at least 3 months in a cool dark place, to allow the incense to mature & blend together to form a complete unit rather than many ingredients.

IT IS DEFINITELY NOT ADVISABLE TO USE ANY OF THE FOLLOWING IN ANY INCENSE OR RITUAL PERFUME:- CANNABIS: FOXGLOVE: DEADLY NIGHTSHADE: HEMLOCK:THORN APPLE: AMANITA MUSCARIA: BLACK HELLEBORE: HENBANE & ANY DERIVATIVE OF THE WHITE POPPY.

Ritual perfumes are used in a similar way to incense, but are applied to the bodies of those participating in the Magickal working. When a group are gathered, their own body scents join with the natural oils & Incense used, to create a totally unique Group identity, that all members of the group will be able to relate to & find their place within.

*CAUTION:* PLEASE REMEMBER;, INCENSE & CHARCOALS ARE A FIRE HAZARD, PLEASE ENSURE THAT INCENSE BURNERS HAVE A LINING OF SAND BEFORE PLACING THE CHARCOAL IN, If your incense Burner has a lid, use it. If you have got a small clay tile to place your incense on, even better, because it will insulate it against you Altar. REMEMBER, EVEN AFTER 4 HOURS, THE CHARCOAL CAN STILL BE VERY HOT, DISPOSE OF. WHERE THEY WILL NOT COMBUST WITH ANYTHING ELSE.

## MAKING RITUAL PERFUMED OILS

To make a ritual perfume, use the recipes for Incense & make up accordingly, take 1oz incense & 25Ml of sweet almond oil (use sweet, ordinary Almond oil is a diuretic!). Crush the incense down to a fine powder, using either a mortar & pestle or a coffee grinder.

Place both in a small pan & apply heat, DO NOT BOIL. Keep at that level for 10 mins watching constantly, let it cool at room temperature, strain & bottle immediately. Use within 3 months in a cool place. If it is to be kept permanently, use Benzoin at 2Ml per 25Ml to act as a preservative. Here follows some examples of Incense formula, all are tried & tested as being effective, & are of no great antiquity, being my sole invention, as a compounder of some note of incenses & Magickal Herbal products.

HORNED GOD INCENSE.
Patchouli leaves   1 part
Golden Rod 1 part
Oak bark      1 part
Myrrh 1 part
Damiana          2 parts
Amber Oil 10ml per 8oz dry herbs

Place all the dry ingredients in an earthenware bowl & cover with the essential oil. Place by an open fire to macerate but do not boil. This is to be carried out in a Dark Moon or a winters Great Sabbat.

WHITE GODDESS INCENSE
Orris Root  1 Part
White Rose petals 1 part
Gum dammar  2 parts
Jasmine Oil 5Ml to 8oz Dry Herb
Neroli oil 5Ml to 8 oz. dry herb

This Incense should be made on the Night of a New Moon. Place all ingredients in a silver bowl, cover with a white cloth & leave to bathe in the light of a full Moon, leave for full Luna cycle.

## ESBAT INCENSE
Damiana  3 parts
Olibanium 2 parts
Rosemary 1 part
Gum Copal 2 parts
Euphorbia 1 part

To be compounded upon the night of a full moon, preferably at a Coven meeting, or if not, at least within a magickal circle. Pound all the ingredients to a fine powder in a Mortar & Pestle.

## *SPECIALIST INCENSES & OILS*

These Incenses & oils are to be used for a specific purpose or intention, do not over use these Incense & oils as they are powerful, both in composition & spirit.

## EXORCISM INCENSE

This is an excellent banishing Incense & should be burned in your workroom prior to you casting a circle, to clear the area of all vibrations, it must be backed up immediately afterwards with an incense of a positive intention, such as a deity incense, such as you will be using in your ritual, to re instill good vibrations into an area.

To make the Incense take equal amounts of Myrrh, camphor, nutmeg, & Mint. Make upon a Sunday. or within the hour of the Sun, making the incense in a vessel of silver.

## SCRYING INCENSE
This is used as an aid to the development of clairvoyancy.
Camphor  4 part
Damiana  5 part
Verbena  2 part
Sandalwood  5 part
Jasmine oil  10ml per 8oz dry herbs

Mix in the hour of mercury, in a vessel of silver or glass.

## INITIATION OIL
Rosemary  3 part
Musk Oil  10ml per 8oz dry herbs

Mandrake  5 part
Frankincense 5 parts Ylang
Ylang Oil 10ml per 8oz dry herbs
Mix upon the night of a full moon & leave to stand in a jar macerating for at least 6 months, strain & bottle, adding Benzoin.

## MAGICKAL BATH PURIFIER
Sea Salt    4 parts
Rue herbs   1 part
Soapwort    1 part
Honeysuckle oil   10ml per 8oz dry herbs
Mix together on the night of a full moon & leave to stand in a jar in a dark place for at least 3 months. use in your pre ritual baths at the rate of one tablespoon per bath.

## MAGICKAL CLEANSING SOLUTION
Chamomile flowers  4oz
Rue herb           4oz
Myrrh resin        2oz
Small piece of Gold & Small piece of silver
1 Iron nail (must be iron not steel)
3 Pint well water (Chalice well at Glastonbury preferred)
Benzoin as preservative 10 drops per finished pint

On the night of a New Moon.  Boil all the herbs, not the Myrrh resin, in with the well water for 4 hours on an open fire, in a pot with the lid closed to keep the liquor in.  Leave to go cold

On the night of a Full Moon strain the liquor off the herbs & add the small piece of silver, also add the Benzoin.  Bottle in a dark bottle (wine bottle).

On the Night of a Waning Moon add the Gold & the iron nail.

Shake well & say.

*" May the blessings of the Lord & Lady be upon this potion, let it cleanse & purify all it comes into contact with & empower with the energies of the Lady of the Moon. So Mote it be!"*

# Chapter 13

# FINAL THOUGHTS & CONCLUSIONS

The intention of this book was to give an insight into a branch of which has been claimed to have been an Occult art for millennia, that of Wicca, which is developing daily into a recognised system of belief, that, through the hard work of it's adherents is moving away from any dubious links with the Occult that is secret & hidden, & for that reason under suspicion, & is quickly re-establishing itself as the indigenous religion of the Isles of Albion.

Like Wicca itself, this book as a concept has also changed & evolved from its early beginning & has gone through a continual change being updated for the fifth time now, it has become a standard work with many Covens on the basic practise of Wicca.

I am not promoting a system of rigidity within this book, the concept of this book is one of freedom, freedom of personal choice & addition from you. It is a concept of communing with the deities of the earth, the Goddess & the Horned God, in your own ways, that way you can contribute to the magick of this book. The idea's & rituals given in this book are only given as a source of inspiration for you, to give you an idea as to their structure, of course you can use the rituals as they stand, but you can also add your own material to them if you so desire.

All of this book has been written from a viewpoint of what may be considered Traditional Gardnerian material, not taken ad verbatim out of the book of Shadows, or by breaking any oaths that I have sworn. The viewpoint is Traditional Gardnerian, the words are my own, I have not cobbled together other authors idea's & passing them off as my own. This book then is a foretaste of a nature religion, to experience the real thing, get out into a natural surrounding such as a wood or a deserted beach beneath a Full Moon on a clear starlit Night & truly open your heart out to the forces that are pulsating all around you & within you. Then you will truly experience the power & the beauty that is the Lord & the Lady of the Old ways. THE GODDESS & HORNED GOD OF THE OLDEN DAYS, who have been since the dawn of time & whose light has been dimmed by the lies of mankind.

By the time that you have reached this far & if you have learned from the contents of this book, you should have some understanding as to the true nature of the natural force that we call Magick! You will have learned that by using & working with this force, you are capable of making things easier for yourself.......or the detriment of others, be it a love spell or a curse. Magick is but a power it has no conscience. THIS IS THE HARD PART....The use of magick is up to you, it is your responsibility how you use it!

There is no sell out of conscience within the Old Religion, no guilt trips or bad hang-ups. The Magickan Aleister Crowley (not a Witch but a wise one nevertheless) stated DO WHAT THOU WILT SHALL BE THE WHOLE OF THE LAW.

What Crowley was getting over to his followers with this Law of Thelema, was, that it is not a case of doing what you want, without thought of the hurt of others that you may cause, but rather do your will (Magick) in recognition of your responsibility. To this end was the response LOVE IS THE LAW; LOVE UNDER WILL.

All Pagans believe in answering for their actions when the time arrives to ascend to a higher plane of consciousness. Not as a guilt trip but as an explanation of what you have done with your time upon this Earth Plane. This is known as the Law Of Karma, which Is basically;-

Any force that you transmit to effect the lives of others will return upon you threefold, whether it is Love or Hate you give, it will return enhanced threefold back! He or she who curses today could be tomorrows victim, is it worth it?

Think & act in a responsible manner & as parting words from me remember;
*Eight words the Witches Rune Fulfils*
*-If it harms None Do as you will*

From one Wise one to another, I wish you as we always wish each other
*A Blessed Be!*

# Other products available from Mandrake Press Ltd.

## THE HORNED GOD
*Keith Morgan*
*KM16 £4.95*

A full analysis into the the importance of the Pagan dualistic approach to deity. Explains why a belief in a God is not a patriarchal curiosity.

## SIMPLE CANDLE MAGICK
*Keith Morgan*
*KM17 £3.50*

Use Candles and Incense to create a magickal environment to harness energies and magickal currents for your personal needs.

## EASY ASTRAL PROJECTION
*Keith Morgan*
*KM18 £3.50*

Astral projection is available to all with a little effort and practice. This book gives the FACTS.

## HOW TO USE A OUIJA BOARD
*Keith Morgan*
*KM19 £3.50*

A no nonsense book dealing with the Ouija board as a practical magickal tool. The truth about Ouija boards and how to use them.

# Other products available from Mandrake Press Ltd.

## DOWSING FOR BEGINNERS
### *Keith MorganKM29 £4.00*

Learn how to dowse, one of the Lost Magickal arts. This book will shows many techniques of Dowsing including dowsing with Pendulums, Divining Rods, Hazel twigs and more. This book contains everything that you need to know to help you to Dowse easily and efficiently. Contains charts to help you to dowse, plus detailed information on how to make your own dowsing equipment.Extensively illustrated.

## HIGH MAGIC'S AID
### *by Scire (Dr Gerald B. Gardner) KM27, £4.95*

A reprint of the famous classic work by Gerald B. Gardner, which in a fiction format depicts very imaginatively and vividly the whole aspect of what Wicca is all about. With this being a total reprint, we also have reproduced all of the illustrations from the original, including the original illustration off the dust-wrapper. This edition also includes a new foreword, written by Patricia Crowther.

## THE TRUTH ABOUT WITCHCRAFT
### *Keith Morgan KM04 £2.50*

Written by a practising witch to allay some of the fears & misconceptions about Wicca & Paganism. This is the ideal book to present to parents, friends & family to explain your beliefs & practices in a very simple way.

## CRYSTAL MAGIC
### *Keith Morgan*
### *KM20 £3.50*

Explores the magickal potential of crystals and how they work within the magickal act. An ideal first book for the student or for those interested in learning more about the use of crystals.

# Other products available from Mandrake Press Ltd.

## MAGICK FOR LOVERS
### Keith Morgan
### KM21 £3.50

Probably the most practical and sensible book on the subject. Full of do's and don'ts and genuine advice from this best-selling author.

## MAKING MAGICKAL INCENSE AND RITUAL PERFUMES
### Keith Morgan
### KM22 £4.95

A simple and concise guide. A wealth of information & accurate recipes for producing your own ritual incenses and perfumes.

## A WITCHES KITCHEN
### Keith Morgan KM24 £3.50

This book show you:
* How to make genuine witches potions, incenses and perfumes
* How to use herbs for magick
* How to plant a herb garden
* How to make incenses and ritual perfumes
* How to dry and store herbs for your incenses . . . and more

## PYRAMID POWER
### Keith Morgan KM25 £7.95

Create your own 'Pyramid Power'. Through this book you will learn how to use the Pyramids so that you can utilise them to work Magick for your own purposes, whatever that purpose may be. You can use the *Pyramid Power Kit* to influence natural Magickal forces to give you advantage over the most desired results, which can be: * Winning lotteries, raffles and the pools * Obtaining a job * Finding someone to love * All of this can be possible with 'Pyramid Power'!

**Other products available from Mandrake Press Ltd.**

## ALTERNATIVE WICCA
### *Keith Morgan KM01 £4.95*

Continuing from *Harmonics of Wicca* - the fourth part in the theology course of Wiccan philosophies. This books explores the alternatives within magickal techniques & practises which are harmonious with the belief system that is Wiccan. An intensive & extremely thought provoking book that may challenge the system that has become established whilst paving the way for the new Aeon that is the birthright of all Pagans !

## THE HARMONICS OF WICCA
### *Keith Morgan KM02 £4.95*

The continuance on from *Wicca Awakens & Traditional Wicca*, it is a Balancing process for the Old Religion in the New Age. Vital & exciting concepts that are occurring within the Craft today. It gets away from the medieval concept of the Craft & goes back to its roots, unifying many Pagan principles within the Craft structures. Extensively illustrated throughout

## SO YOU WANT TO BE A WITCH
### *Keith Morgan KM06 £3.50*

Explains in a simple & often light hearted format what it is to be a Witch, whether witches are born or made, whether the perceptions one holds about witches is correct (often it is not!) This book is a valuable asset to aid your in your search for the true path.

## HAVE YOU BEEN CURSED?
### *Keith Morgan*
### *KM03 £3.50*

A serious study into the phenomena of curses & hexes. Contains much vital information for people who think they may be at the receiving end of a curse.

# Other products available from Mandrake Press Ltd.

## RUNE MAGICK
### Keith Morgan KM12 £3.50

*Rune Magick* has been written for the beginner and explores the history of the runes, the ways of divination as well as the ways of magickal invocations, spells, bindrunes etc that can be created with runic scripts. Contains much information about the nature of each individual runestave, not found elsewhere.

## ARADIA:
### Gospel of the Witches
### C G Leland   KM11 £4.95

*Aradia,* first published in the late 19th Century, aroused a great deal of interest. The first source book of the Old Religion. The information in the book contains a great deal of ritual material for today's pagans.

## SIMPLE SPELLS FROM A WITCHES SPELLBOOK
### Keith Morgan   KM15 £3.50

*Simple spells from a Witches spellbook* is the kind of beginners book that has been so needed. Excellent advice for all.

## READ THE TAROT WITHIN 7 DAYS
### Keith Morgan  KM14 £3.50

This extremely simple book shows how to read the tarot in a very effective & simple manner, the way tarot should be read, in relating the individual to their circumstances. Absolutely ideal for anyone having a minimal knowledge of the tarot.

# Other products available from Mandrake Press Ltd.

## CANNABIS: A USER'S GUIDE
*Anya Marika  KM30 £5.00*

The definitive users guide to Cannabis, including essential information on how to:
- Roll Joints.
- Use a Pipe or Waterpipe.
- Smoke Grass and Hashish.
- How to Eat and Drink Cannabis.
- Plus much more.

## CANNABIS: A GROWERS GUIDE
*Anya Marike KM28 £5.00*

All the vital information needed to study the practise of growing cannabis in temperate climates. Focusing on the biology and botany of the cannabis plants, it also goes into the vital chemistry needed to enable such projects to be viable. This book is sold on the strict understanding that it is to be used for educational purposes only and not to be used for criminal acts.

## COOKING WITH CANNABIS
*Anya Marika  KM31 £5.00*

How to use Cannabis in cooking both for social and medical purposes.

Includes information on the correct methods of cooking Cannabis for maximum efficiency.

Includes recipes for all manner of Cannabis based dishes.

## THE MAGICKAL RECORD
*Keith Morgan  KM05 £3.50*

This unique book with its pre-printed format allows you to quickly record your rituals. All the information contained within will be personalised by you, So keeping a record of your successful spells (or not so successful!) really is a matter of minutes rather than hours.

## Other products available from Mandrake Press Ltd.

# TRADITIONAL WICCA
### *Keith Morgan   KM07 £4.95*

The complimentary volume to *Wicca Awakens;* explores the subjects raised to greater depths - the true nature & identity of the Old Religions of these lands, the use of natural magickal techniques, ritual & legends based on Coven teachings. Together with the first in its series, *Wicca Awakens,* & its follower, the *Harmonics of Wicca, Traditional Wicca* makes a complete set of course-work. Extensively illustrated.

# MAKING MAGICKAL TOOLS & RITUAL EQUIPMENT
### *Keith Morgan   KM08 £3.50*

This book gives the reader all the information needed for making ritual magickal tools, including making, Athames; Swords, pentacles, Robes, Incenses Oils & Much Much more with easy to follow instructions, using raw materials & tools that are readily available. Extensively illustrated.

# PLANET MAGICK
### *Keith Morgan   KM09 £4.00*

Planets influence our lives in a myriad of ways, our moods, our emotions, our feelings. This book shows how to harness this power & channel it to bring about effects on our everyday circumstances. Explains in depth, planetary correspondences, & how to create your own planetary rituals.